Rangoon and Back

Ron Dudley

Old Bakehouse Publications

Abertillery

First published in August 2007

ISBN 978 1 905967 02 5

Published in the U.K. by
Old Bakehouse Publications
Church Street,
Abertillery, Gwent NP13 1EA
Telephone: 01495 212600 Fax: 01495 216222
Email: theoldbakeprint@btconnect.com
Website: www.oldbakehouseprint.co.uk

Made and printed in the UK
by J.R. Davies (Printers) Ltd.

British Library Cataloguing in Publication Data: a catalogue
record for this book is available from the British Library.

Foreword

Ron Dudley has a gift, he smiles through adversity and takes others along for the ride. If you're looking for a Wilbur Smith type novel, this isn't the book for you. That said, if you're looking for an account of the last days of the Burma Campaign as seen through the eyes of a young man with a wicked sense of humour, read on.

As one of the fortunate generation I can't what horrors those who fought and those who died fighting the Japanese must have endured. Steaming jungles, monsoons and a threat just as deadly as their enemy, disease.

Much of this has been described in books written by their leaders and every other rank you can think of, but this little gem speaks volumes for the ordinary man. The blokes who got on with the job in hand, ordinary men who lost their youth as they fought and died alongside each other. Yet through all the horrors of war, this is a story about a generation of young men who could still find the time to laugh at themselves.

Pete Flowers
Sutton,
Suffolk.

Forewarned: Author's Note

This book *'The Road to Rangoon and Back'* is not meant to be a concise historical document of the last days of the Japanese occupation of Burma but also a collection of humorous situations that myself and others found themselves in. I must confess that my memory does sometimes get a little confused with my imagination and for this I apologise. Some of the accounts of those situations, as true as they are however, are not intended to offend in any way and if they do, then please again accept my apologies. The real intention is for these little stories to bring a smile to the reader's lips which I hope they will and I thank you for your kind deliberation.

Born in 1925 and brought up in the End of London having a primary education he left school in August 1939 and went to work in a factory to be trained as a fitter. After one month in September 1939 war was declared against Nazi Germany. He went through the London Blitz. In March 1944 he was called up to serve as a Wireless Operator with the Royal Corps of Signals. Serving in Burma and India with South East Asia Command he returned to Blighty to be demobbed in December 1947. One year later in December 1948 he married Evelyn Scott after one year's engagement. After two years in a factory the couple moved to Suffolk, he taking up employment as a farm labourer and they were now living in a 400 year old tied cottage. After one year in Suffolk the couple moved to Essex into another tied cottage. He was now employed as a cowman and now living in Great Bardfield in a council bungalow. He then returned to life in a factory in Great Dunmow, then moving into a more lucrative job in Chelmsford Essex being trained as a toolmaker, driving 20 miles to work every day. There followed another change of direction moving to South Wales taking up employment with a pen making factory in Crumlin. He retired in 1990 at the age of 65 years. The couple have resided in South Wales now for over 40 years and have made many friends there. Ron kept racing pigeons for 26 years and writes for the pigeon journal the British Homing World under the pseudonym of Jerry Attric.

Dedication

To my wife and mate of sixty years Evelyn. A companionship built on LOVE, LOYALTY and TRUST neither of us ever wavering. THE ENTIRE SUM OF EXISTENCE IS THE MAGIC OF BEING NEEDED BY JUST ONE PERSON.
Also to my parents. My mother Helen who must have suffered so much pain when giving birth to me and my dad Albert who left me his humour. Bless you both and my late brother Les whom I miss so much.

Chapter One

'The Beginning of the Road'

A shrill scream rang out from the bedroom of 24 Exmouth Road a two-storey terraced house in Walthamstow in the East End of London. Neighbours had gathered outside listening to the intermittent screams that had been going on for some time. Wondering what was happening to that poor woman in the front bedroom.

A window was thrown open, and a large lady called down. *'It's an eleven, and a half pound baby boy.'*

The lady was our next door neighbour Mrs Simmons. The new born baby was myself on the first day of May 1925. When my mother Nellie was reaching for the time of my entrance to this world, the poor woman was five feet two inches in height and weighed just six and a half stone. Yes! just ninety one pounds shedding practically twelve percent of her weight. Me $11^1/2$ pounds in my stockinged feet. It must have been like a cork popping out from a bottle of champagne. The mid-wife struggling to hold me up to smack my bottom, and me threatening to have her on an assault charge if she laid a hand on me. So she dropped me on my Uncle Ned (head) and I've never recovered.

Can't say I remember much of my early years until I started infant school at Queens Road. There I had my first crush on a shapely little blonde whose father had a general grocery shop also selling newspapers.

She showed no interest in me whatsoever. A right toffee-nosed bit of crumpet. So our affair was never consummated, our ways separated, and at the age of eight I went to a junior school called Mission Grove. Memories of that place are a bit vague. I can't remember any of the names of my classmates or teachers.

Then, at eleven years of age, I finished up at one of the roughest schools in Walthamstow, Mark House Road. A rather large school with I suppose two hundred pupils and a very tough teaching staff. The headmaster was Mr Woolfe. A bloody masochist who delighted in inflicting pain on his pupils. Every boy dreaded being sent to Mr Woolfe's study to be caned. One such boy was sent there and he ran away. They found him floating in the River Lea drowned.

His mother turned up at the school some time afterwards with a sturdy umbrella. Locking herself in his study with the bastard, she gave him some of his own medicine. No criminal charges were ever brought against her.

So moving on to my own favourite character Mr 'Dickie' Palmer the poetry master. An elderly man wearing drain pipe trousers. The reason for his nickname was the fact that he would have both hands in his trouser pockets playing pocket billiards or re-arranging his tackle.

I can see Dickie now reading his favourite poem *'The Ploughman'*. I'm trying to paint a picture of him striding up and down in front of the class. He walked a bit like Groucho Marx, but with his drainpiped legs further apart, taking very long strides. Hands deep into his pockets cupping his tackle, he would recite *'The Ploughman striding lank following the plough'*. He would face the blackboard and if he heard someone talking, he would take aim over his shoulder and hit the culprit on his loaf of bread (head).

There were other colourful characters on the teaching staff such as Mr Smith the geography master. A fairly large man with a gigantic belly. It came off his chest like a slide. We heard that it was brought on when he was in Africa drinking contaminated water. I enjoyed his lessons they intrigued me with tales of Zulus and Pygmies. So much so I would spend hours in our local library reading about Africa and the tribes of that continent.

There was Mr Newton the science master, and then a large red faced corpulent bastard by the name of 'Eggie' Watson. He was our teacher with his shiny bald head, and Charles Laughton rubbery lips dribbling when he had a frightened boy shivering in front of him waiting to be caned.

There were all sorts of gimmicks to get the cane to slide off your hand with soap and potato juice. If you lowered your hand as he brought the instrument of torture down or curved your fingers downwards so it slid off, he would place your hand on top of his desk palm upwards, and WHOOSH! your hand would be trapped between the cane and the desk.

The author in his school uniform with his mum Helen.

Did it do any good? I cannot remember any boy not leaving Mark House Road who didn't know his three 'Rs'. All could read all could write and all could add up.

There is one other master who comes to mind, the music man Mr Cook, a tall thin man. On those cold frost-bitten mornings when the bell had rung and we were all formed up ready to be marched to our classrooms, he would creep between the rows of boys. If you were talking or giggling, he had a rolled up copy of the *Radio Times* with which he would catch you with a resounding whack round your frost-bitten ear'ole.

Again I must confess I really enjoyed his music lessons. Of course it was all classical music. Wagner, Beethoven, Mozart, Bizet etc. I loved the Overtures, The Barber of Seville, The Thieving Magpie and so on.

I went onto jazz when I left school, but Cookie introduced me to music.

So let's meet some of the wonderful neighbours in Exmouth Road. Our houses backed onto the dead centre of Walthamstow, the cemetery. Originally it was surrounded by a broken down fence, but was then replaced by a high breeze blocked wall with broken glass cemented in the top to keep us kids out. When the fence was there we would bunk over, and look for snails and sometimes find a tortoise. These would be under the old gravestones leaning against the fence.

We were caught by the man in charge once. Les my brother was climbing back over the fence and he grabbed him by one leg and my brother pissed his trousers. I called my Mum (as stated a very small woman), but she put the frighteners up that bloke.

So to our neighbours. Next door going downwards were Mr and Mrs Simmons with their two boys Freddie the eldest and my mate Dougie who was a year younger than myself.

Going up the street next door were Mr and Mrs Cheshire, an elderly couple. Mr Cheshire like my Dad Albert, and Mr Simmons had fought in WWI. Mr Cheshire would show me photographs of men in putties wrapped round their legs waiting to go into the trenches. Surely a war that should have stopped all wars with the terrible carnage and waste of young lives on both sides.

Sunday mornings George Cheshire would sit down at his upright piano and thump out those old ballads. *'Its a long way to Tipperary,' 'Keep the home fires burning', 'Pack up your troubles in your old kit bag'*. His wife Kate Cheshire was a very sad lady. They had a daughter Ivy who died in infancy. Mrs Cheshire kept Ivy's clothes in an old chest, and would take them out and wash and iron them at regular intervals as if she were still alive. So sad.

To the far side of them were the Tomkins an older couple. Mr Tomkins had songbirds in wooden cages on the side of the brick walls and in the spring they would sing their hearts out. I went into their house many times and was fascinated by the glass-fronted cabinets on the walls filled with exotic coloured butterflies mounted with a pin through their thorax; little knowing that I would be helping someone in the jungles of Burma collecting those glamourous insects.

Moving on up the road was another family whose youngest son had the nickname of 'Hardbake'. He stunk of excreta probably because he didn't wipe his bum properly after he'd been to the bog (captain's log).

We had a game called 'Jimmy, Jimmy, Knacker'. You would have two teams of say eight each side. If 'Hardbake' was playing when the captain picked his team he would be the last selected.

Now the leading boy would bend down in front of a wall with his hands braced against it. The next boy would put his head between this boys legs and the others in the team would follow suit. Like a scrummage in rugby union but one behind each other. So you had a line of boys all bent over coming out from the wall.

If 'Hardbake' was in your team he would be the last down for obvious reasons. Who would want to stick his head between his legs? When they were ready and had braced themselves, the opposing team would vault one at a time over the other team's backs. They would then jump up and down to try and force their opponents to collapse. The team underneath would shout *'Jimmy Jimmy Knacker One Two Three I Spy Acker She'*. They would shout this three times, and if they hadn't collapsed it was their turn to jump on the other team's backs. If 'Hardbake' was in your team you would let him go first. Chances were the other team after their nostrils were assaulted by the cack in his strides, would break ranks.

Opposite our house there was a road at right angles to ours and on the corner of the two was the family Salmon. Dad Charlie, Mum Elsie and their children Johnnie, Buckle, Katie and their youngest Eddie. A star in the making.

Mrs Salmon was a tousled ginger-haired lady with a very large wart on her face and a moustache to match. She had the most wicked temper. All would be quiet in our street when the Salmon's door would burst open and one of their offspring's eyes bulging with fear, legging it for their life. In hot pursuit a very irate Elsie admonishing her child with a scream of *'Wait till I catch you. You little bastard'*.

She would then perform the most athletic feat. The hunter and quarry would be running in circles. Elsie would be in worn down high heel shoes with stockings round her ankles. As she was running without stopping, she would remove one of her shoes smoothly and take unerring aim clouting her prey a resounding THWACK! round the ear'ole followed by the other shoe. This exhibition would usually finish in tears from both parties until the next time.

Chapter Two

'Moving On'

So moving on. When I left school at Mark House Road in 1939 it was August, and within one month we were at war with Hitler's Nazi Germany. At the top of our road the 'blackshirts' used to meet in a small building. Sir Oswald Mosley would turn up now and again. When war was declared the people in our road broke all the windows in their headquarters and they scarpered.

At the end of the road on the opposite corner was a grocery shop owned by a Belgian. On the pavement outside was a french letter (condom) disposal machine and we would hang about watching who bought the froggies when it got dark. On the other corner was an off-licence owned by Fred Dowell who thought this machine was disgusting.

War had just started and Mr Deleus the owner of the grocery shop was burning some cardboard boxes. Fred Dowell came out from his off-licence brandishing a revolver wanting to lynch the grocer saying he was signalling the Germans. The poor bugger moved away.

When we left school most of us joined a Youth Club situated in Walthamstow High Street. It was Marsh Street School. It had everything to keep you off the street. A full size snooker table, badminton hall, table tennis plus a large lounge where you could enjoy classical music and jazz. I had joined the club not knowing what to expect. There were two main Boy's Clubs; George Gascoigne ex-pupils from a secondary school and Mark House Road ex-pupils from a primary school also a couple of girls clubs. Surprising how many of the boys and girls paired off to get married in later life as my wife Evelyn and I did.

I did fall in love again. A bit one sided as the girl wasn't a bit interested in me. I suppose my main problem was stature as I wasn't very tall. In other words my arse was too near the ground. To be honest at that age in our early teens we were more interested in having a laugh and playing sport.

Most of us got called up or volunteered for one of the fighting branches of the Forces. One such was a thin lad Lennie Newman who joined the Airborne Division against our advice. He was in the Glider Force that landed in Arnhem and never came back. They say the glider he was in crash-landed and the occupants were all killed.

Another, George Davy, was a rear gunner in the Royal Air Force and bought it on his scheduled last flight over Germany.

Then there was Harry Hasler another who volunteered for the Paratroopers. He was reported missing believed killed. Fortunately Harry turned up when peace was declared having been a POW (prisoner of war).

Another lad I went to school with, who lived a couple or doors down in Exmouth Road was Wally Solomans who came out of the Kate Karney very disillusioned, and joined the communists as several others did. Wally was a very intelligent lad. He would rabbit on about the proletariat which was way above my vocabulary. I don't think it lasted long as he settled down and got married.

I must mention another one of us who was always up to playing jokes. We would go off to the local slipper baths to have a proper bath as there were no bathrooms in our houses in those days. You would all go in and pay a small sum receive your soap and towel then wait your turn. There were probably a dozen private cubicles, the place full of steam. You would have been allocated a number and after the attendant had cleaned your particular cubicle, he would call your number out. Take your clobber off put it on the bench seat and try the water with your toe, and slide into the warm water. If it wasn't to your liking you would call out your cubicle number for either cold or hot water.

This is where our prankster would come in, name of Derek Perkins. If he was in number ten he would call out. *'Cold in number six'*, and while you were wallowing in your bath a deluge of ice cold water would hit you.

We used to go on Firewatch on Friday nights at the Club. Usually this meant playing cards into the early hours of Saturday mornings upstairs in the Youth Club. We used to sleep in the library on the ground floor in the divided areas where the readers would study. Our beds were just a few inches off the floor with a single blanket and sheets.

One night Harry Hasler had gone to bed early. Now Harry was a swanky dresser and he had long sideburns growing down his cheeks. After he had got his Uncle Ned (head) down for a while, Perkins crept downstairs. He went into the library part and got himself a couple of those sticky sheets that they put into the books to stamp the return date on.

When Harry was laying on his back, Perkins placed one of these self adhesive sheets each side of his head. In the morning poor old Harry had them stuck to his sideburns and he had to tear half his hair off to remove them.

Derek Perkins worked in a woodyard and the owner was a Fascist so friend Perkins daubed 'Zeig Heil' everywhere.

Some nights in the main hall there would be a dance; Strictly Ballroom. Music from 78rpm records and we would watch one of the members give an exhibition with his partner. I never realised I would watch Nat Horwitz give this same exhibition in a Forces Club in India in several years time.

I used to go into the lounge to listen to record recitals of classical music by a member. I couldn't relate to some of the music when it got too deep, but most of it I did appreciate.

I suppose amongst the Mark House Road boys I was an odd one out as I cannot remember anyone of them being there.

I wandered into the lounge one night and some of the Athan members were listening to jazz. This was New Orleans, Dixieland and Chicago which I was virtually unfamiliar with. They didn't take too much notice of me, one of the Mark House Road boys. I was fascinated by the music. They would put a disc on and mime as if they were playing the solo instruments. I couldn't help tapping my feet to the rhythms. I got to know the names of the instrumentalists. Louis Armstrong, Benny Goodman, Artie Shaw and Duke Ellington.

I found out where they purchased their 78rpm records from, a shop in Hoe Street. You went into this record shop and were given several catalogues. Parlophone, HMV, Decca. From these you would order your records without hearing them. A bit of a gamble. Mum would make me take our old wind-up record player upstairs to play my records. She called it jungle music. After a while the other jazz lovers accepted me as a hanger-on I suppose.

I was working in a factory on war work in Blackhorse Lane Walthamstow and we had a lad working there nicknamed 'Laughing Boy'. He was a loner, never mixing with the other boys. Never a smile on his face, a right misery. I managed to get talking to him and found to my surprise he was a jazz lover. His name was Sid Schooling and we became good mates. He lived in Chingford and I would catch the bus to visit him and listen to our records. He never had much to say for himself but we found a lot in common with our love of jazz. Sid did have a dry sense of humour at times, but always delivered with his straight face.

We had many welders in the factory and amongst them was a young girl from Belgium who was going out with one of the lads in the welding section. She fell pregnant and they planned to get married as you did in those days, honouring the girl. They came round for a collection to buy them a wedding present. When they got to 'Laughing Boy' his comment was why didn't they have a collection a few months before and bought the couple a decent french letter (condom). It would have been a lot cheaper all-round.

If there had been an air raid the night before, there would sometimes be people missing in the morning and word would go round if they hadn't survived. One such victim was a friend of my brother Les. He used to cycle to work from Leyton. At the top of Mark House Road there was a crossroads with Hoe Street, quite a wide junction with traffic lights. A landmine dropped there flattening everything and the friend of my brother must have been there at the wrong time. There were no remains found of anyone including a trolley bus with passengers on it going home from work.

I was on night work grinding welded metal frames for wireless sets. A dirty very noisy job. I had to do it down the far end of the shop. Apart from a small incendiary device, the factory suffered no bombing. If it had been hit I would probably have been the only survivor isolated on my Todd Sloan (own) at the far end of the shop. It wasn't all gloom. We would make dummy hand guns, usually a piece of conduit screwed to a shaped wooden handle and this included the Foremen as well.

Someone would bang a hammer down onto a metal bench and everyone would dive for cover, drawing their dummy guns and banging on the benches. It sounded like the gunfight at the OK Corral. It would just last a few minutes, and it relieved some of the tension of the Blitz and the news of how the war was going.

Hitler's army was now getting a bit thin on the ground, occupying so many countries with an army of occupation in each one. He was now in the Channel Isles. Then he made his biggest mistake by opening another war front in North Africa. Of course he now had the Italians and Mussolini with him, but I don't think the Italian peoples hearts were in the war. Then the Americans started knocking hell out of Germany with their Flying Fortresses and of course the undercover armies all over Europe. Then the Allies landed in Normandy with the might of the USA war machine. The Japanese had captured many of the Pacific Islands and were on the doorstep of India having captured Burma.

It was at this stage that they got in touch with me to take over the campaign in South East Asia with my mate Sir William (Bill) Slim. So read on...

Two thousand of us squaddies embarked from Liverpool on the *'Tegelberg'*, a modern liner designed for the mail run across the Atlantic to America. We sailed up the Mersey, destination unknown; to us anyway just hoping the captain knew the way.

The convoy was a rag tag collection of troop ships, freighters and the Royal Navy, mainly frigates, but we didn't see too much of them en-route. We sailed southwards through the Irish Sea heading for the Bay of Biscay. I was a member of a Royal Corps of Signals contingent. A Cockney landlubber having my first experience of the ocean and ocean-going boats as most of us were.

We were issued with Mae Wests. A bit like two small cushions taped together with another tape to go round your chest. You were ordered to carry them with you wherever you were, a wise precaution in case we were torpedoed etc. Now one of our motley members of the Signals was a young lad who didn't have a clue how to cope in the big wide world. He was all of six feet tall. His legs were half the length of his gangling body. The rest of him had just been thrown together with what was left over at the end of a shift yet he was a Bachelor of Science. We were also issued with a hammock to hoist onto pipes that ran along the decks below.

So most of us managed to get our hammocks tied round the pipes and that was the easy part. The hard part was getting into them. Poor old 'Lofty' was snookered. The lights had been dimmed just enough so you could see your way to the toilet. The long one had by now got his hammock over the pipes and finished mounting it like a horse. Remember the instruction to keep your Mae West with you at all times (for those not familiar with a Mae West it is a life saving device to keep you afloat if the boat sunk). Lofty had taken this literally and wore his at all times.

Here we all are watching him and some falling out of our hammocks. In the end a half dozen of us laid his hammock flat on the deck, laid Lofty on it still with his life jacket on and pulled him up. This wasn't the end of him and his Mae West, he even wore it when he went for a shave slashing it to ribbons. If he had jumped into the drink he would have sunk like a stone.

When they finally amputated his life jacket from him he had a thick dirt mark where the line of the jacket had been and a long goat's beard.

Chapter Three

'The London Blitz'

How did I manage to find myself embarking to Far East in early 1945? Born in the East End of London in 1925 one of two brothers. At fourteen years four months I left school in August 1939 with just a primary education and found myself working in a factory. I had been wearing long trousers for a year and when I started work, my parents bought me a dark blue boiler suit. I was a bit of a short arse. The legs and arms were about six inches too long and had to be turned up. The body length of the boiler suit was again a foot too long and the crutch was across my knees.

In September Dad, Mum and us two boys were listening to Neville Chamberlain telling us we were now in a state of war with Hitler's Germany. It didn't mean a lot to a fourteen-year-old boy.

The factory went on war work and women came in to be welders, turners, millers etc., and the men were getting called up for service. A gang of men came to our terraced house dug a large hole at the bottom of the garden and sank an Anderson Shelter into the hole; the dirt they dug out finishing on top of the shelter. Our house was terraced rented property backing onto the local rest camp Walthamstow Cemetery. We were to spend a year in our corrugated bedroom. Lord Haw-Haw used to come on the air telling us *'to get down your rat holes'*.

It was come home from work, get changed and wash. Have your nosh then down into our submerged tin shed when the sirens sent us scurrying. We would lay there listening to the Luftwaffe raining their death load onto a defenceless target. Then the anti-aircraft guns arrived stationed on open ground firing their shells at the bombers. If you ventured out you were likely to be decapitated by the shrapnel from the exploded shells. Large slivers of white hot cast metal from the casings of the shells. Another line of our defences were the large silver barrage balloons manned by the RAF.

I remember one Sunday the Germans started coming over in droves. It was at lunch time and I was visiting a friend who had moved a couple of miles away. The bombers were in tight formation heading for the docks which they pounded for 48 hours. They had fighter cover. Our fighters came after them Hurricanes and Spitfires. Vastly outnumbered, but diving through the middle of the German formation. If they shot one down they would do a victory roll, low over the houses with the people in the streets waving and cheering. Another hazard were the land mines. Parachuted down and exploding downwards when they touched a building flattening whole large areas.

I was doing two nights fire watching. One night at the Youth Club and one up the top of our road in the school. Mainly we were watching for incendiary bombs falling in sticks. Things did quieten down a bit and I started courting the tea girl at work. We were also using the Youth Club more. If there was a raid it was a bit hairy coming home with the bombs falling and the shrapnel raining down.

Chapter Four
'Call Up'

I reached my eighteenth birthday and had to report for my medical at Whipps Cross Hospital. We were seated on long wooden benches waiting to be called out to be inspected by one of the team of doctors brandishing stethoscopes. You were all in your birthday suits not knowing where to put your hands. You had to give a urine sample (not in those pretty little bottles with the screw tops you get now). The bottles were all shapes and sizes with labels stuck on the sides for you to put your name on. As your name was called out the doctor would order 'Bend over' and he would go on to examine every orifice in your body. Then he would check your manhood. 'Cough!'. I suggested he took a step backwards as we didn't want any accidents. (Joking).

I then had a letter telling me to report to Canterbury Barracks in Kent in March 1944. I was eighteen years and nine months. The family came to see me off including the girlfriend who was all in tears, promising to wait till the end of time for my return.

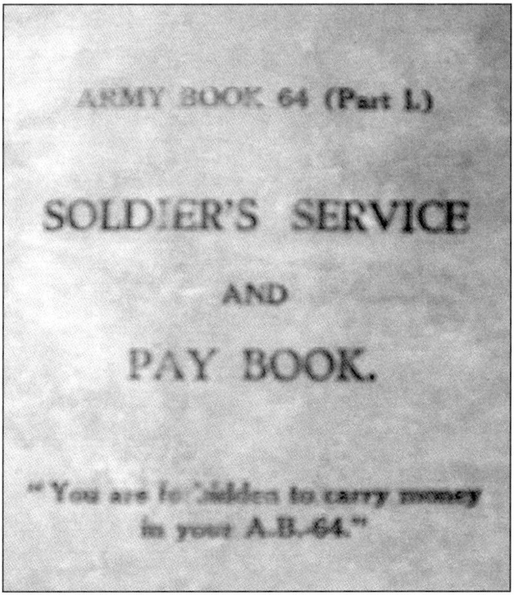

So I arrived at Canterbury railway station and myself with others were taken to the barracks and allocated a barrack room. It being a Nissen hut. We were issued with our hairy uniforms, boots and gaiters and a best friend your .303 rifle. We were given the weekend off to take our civilian clothes home; I suppose we all felt proud in our uniforms.

My girlfriend who was going to wait till the end of time had run out of patience and was now going with a mate! Some mate, some girlfriend. Scrubber! Returning to Canterbury there were a few who had gone AWOL a bit disenchanted with the Kate Carney (army). To be perfectly honest I was looking forward to my new life. I felt equipped to look after myself.

I decided early on to keep a low profile and just be one of the squad that I now found myself in. We were taught how to lay our bed out in the morning, our blankets folded neatly, kit laid out tidy, spare boots polished and rifle kept spotless including the barrel. And so on the Rifle Range with your best friend getting acquainted.

Our Sergeant showed us how to creep up on the enemy using dead ground and of course how to march. Mainly discipline at all times. I seemed to have got through all this initial training without drawing attention to myself. The main exercise was to sit you in front of a selection board to decide your best prospects as a soldier. I was fascinated how they selected you for the unit you were going to be sent to.

If you had been trained as a greengrocer in civvy street you would probably finish up in the Royal and Electrical Engineers. If you were being trained before you enlisted as an engineer you would be cook material. Whatever you had been trained as in civilian life forget it. They wanted you to do it Army Style.

So what had they got for me as I had started life out in engineering. We all had IQ tests, but the one that fascinated me was when you sat in front of a record machine put some headphones on and they put on a record. All you could hear was a series of dashes and dots which you wrote down on a pad. Was this a hearing test? No way!

Out of about thirty of us I was the only one selected for the Royal Corps of Signals to be trained as a Wireless Operator. So I found myself dispatched to the Royal Corps of Signals in Catterick. The depot consisted of large storeyed buildings and I found myself in 56 squad. Probably two dozen of us to become Operators Wireless and Line (OW/L). The course was to last six months and we were taught how to operate a wireless set, to read and send the Morse Code up to eighteen words a minute progressing to thirty words as you got more proficient.

They attempted to get you to all pronounce your diction the same. The reason being if you were in a Regiment or Division and were sending a message using speech or R. Toch as the army called it. If you had a definite accent the enemy interception could pick you up and follow your unit wherever you started broadcasting.

The man who had the job of getting us to all speak the same was a small studious looking Sergeant with army issue metal rimmed glasses. Our squad had Scousers from Liverpool, Geordies from Newcastle, Brummies from Birmingham and of course my cockney accent from London.

He gave us a Call Sign Able, Baker, Charlie and he went round the room. I was going to say tearing his hair out, but he was completely bald. So he got to me and I called out in what I thought was perfectly good English. He looked at me in disbelief and repeated my accent. *'Eyeball, Biker, Charlie'*. He was on a no win situation.

There were probably twenty or so squads at Catterick at the same time as ours in different stages of the six months course. Our main challenge was to learn the Morse Code. There were Nissen huts lined up down this avenue and if you walked between them you would hear twenty or so male voices calling out in unison *'Dee-Daa'*. This being the letter *'A'* Dot Dash. You would be sat in front of a morse key with your index finger on the knob at the top. The instructors key would be wired to all the learners keys and would go down as he pressed his.

The Corporal in charge of our squad was a Full Corporal who had seen action in North Africa and wore his Eighth Army ribbons with pride. He was an Irishman through and through with a broad Irish brogue. He had a side cap worn at a jaunty angle and somehow his uniform always looked like a civilian suit. He also walked with a jaunty swagger and he was a 'Piss Artist'. Corporal Paddy Burgess would go out weekends with a Sergeant friend drinking and would stagger into the barrack room in the early hours of Monday morning stoned out of his mind.

All the squads of maybe twenty would parade on the big square Monday morning for roll call. Our second in command of the squad was a Lance Corporal Tony Mercer who I shall talk about some time later in these memoirs.

The order would ring out. 'Squads report'. This meant reporting absentees, sick etc. It would get to 'Fifty Six Squad'. Complete silence. Paddy doing his upmost to stand upright. L/Cpl Mercer would take over. *'One absent, one sick,* and dropping his voice. *One pissed'*. So we passed out after sitting all our tests. They tagged one signalman who had been at Catterick for a whole year to pass the six months course.

It being 'Lofty' that I began this saga with in the first instance of this narrative. Paddy made him stand some distance from our squad. We were in full battle dress, the lot, with big pack on your back which had to be hitched as high as you could get it. Poor old 'Lofty's was down on his arse like a parachute. We were sent to Crash Camp in Northumberland near Morpeth not too far from the border with Scotland. The plan to toughen us up for combat. We learnt how to down ten pints of beer in one session and some close combat with the women.

We then found ourselves back in Yorkshire in an old cotton mill with low beamed ceilings. Tony Mercer turned up there having volunteered and I got to know him better. After some more toughening up drinking sessions, we were called on parade one morning and told that a draft of two thousand were to be sent overseas. There were two thousand and six of us and they took the six youngest off and my name was read out.

It was now Christmas 1944 and they billeted us in an old broken down Manor House about six miles from Huddersfield. We were taken in by lorry to work in the town's post office sorting room. I had finished my shift and had a couple of hours to spare so I wandered into that marvellous institution the Salvation Army canteen. I had a cup of Rosie Lee (tea) and a wad (cake). I had noticed while walking through town the RAOC dance band was performing in one of the cinemas. Nearly every unit had a Big Band and the Blue Rockets were one of the more famous.

So here am I warming my nose up in a cup of boiling tea when about twenty soldiers walked in with their instruments in their leather cases. I guessed who they were in their dress hats which incidentally are similar colours to the Signals. Oxford and Cambridge Blue and I had mine on.

After they finished their tea one of them approached me asking if I knew the whereabouts of the cinema they were appearing in. I volunteered to show them where it was. This one lad fell in beside me and he confirmed they were indeed the RAOC Blue Rockets and he played trombone. (Royal Army Ordnance Corps)

We arrived at their destination and my new found friend asked *'Are you coming in to see the show?'* I explained I was borasic lint (skint). He told me to mix with the band and I went through the Stage Door to their dressing room finishing up in the wings of the stage.

I was given a cup of tea and biscuit by one of the lady singers and really enjoyed this unexpected pleasure. Standing in the wings I could see the audience. So the show finished. I went back to the band's dressing room, and thanked them all for their hospitality and wandered out from the stage door into the Huddersfield night. I had half an hour to spare before the lorry came to pick us up and was just mooching along looking into the shop windows when this not unattractive girl sidled up. I can remember it was outside a photographers which has no bearing on my story at all.

'Are you a member of the Blue Rockets dance band?' I let her carry on. *'I've just been to see the show and I saw you in the wings'*. I thought hello son your away here. *'Well I am one of the vocalists and have a slight cold so I had a night off tonight. Can I escort you home?'* She replied *'I have to catch a bus at the depot'*. She slipped her arm through mine and we arrived at the depot. We had a bit of a snog then her bus arrived. What she did next I could not believe it. She snatched my hat from my Uncle Ned (head) and mounted the stairs to the upper deck. I gave chase and caught the bus. I climbed the stairs and there was this bird clutching her trophy from the night, my titfer (tit for tat - hat), I managed to extricate it from her grasp (she wasn't half strong), blessed her as you do in this sort of situation, and jumped off the bus. Finding myself a couple of miles outside the town and by the time I had walked back, the lorry had left and I had a six mile walk to our digs. That night I swore never to tell 'Porkies' (pork pies - lies) again.

I was finally put on a draft and we were given two weeks embarkation leave. Now there was this beautiful natural blonde that lived round the corner from our house. Way out of my league. I being just a common fitter working on the shop floor of a factory and her being an office girl at another firm.

I went to this dance at her place of employment. By now my uniform had moulded itself to me and I looked the part. There was Lily at the dance. Never being a shy lad I sauntered over and asked her for this quick-step. I had learned to dance and having a natural sense of rhythm I could get round the floor without treading all over my partner's feet. To my surprise she accepted. Probably didn't recognise that scruff from Exmouth Road. She melted in my arms as we glided across the floor losing ourselves in the moment. How about that from an illiterate squaddie! By now she had twigged me. I spent the rest of the evening getting to know Lily and we seemed to gel. I took her home as I said just round the corner from our house.

We kissed goodnight. Nothing passionate just a gentle caress of our lips. Hers were like velvet. I spent the rest of my leave with Lily and I couldn't believe my luck as she had several older brothers who were into jazz and big band music.

I would take my 78rpm records and we would listen to the Dorsey Bros., Glen Miller, Duke Ellington etc., and we would say good-night on her doorstep and she let me know from the start - no groping, just tender kisses. She wrote many letters to me over 10 months, then she informed me she was going out with another fellow whom she married. He became the youngest mayor of Walthamstow. Thank you Lily for your friendship from over sixty years ago.

Chapter Five

'On Our Way to India'

Two thousand of us embarked on the *'Tegelberg'* from Liverpool as stated previously sailing up the Mersey to the Far East. Down through the Irish Sea slipping past the English Channel into the Bay of Biscay with its bad reputation. As it was the sea was kind to us. Some of us seemed to get our sea legs sooner than others, I being one of the lucky ones. A lot of the draft took some time to get used to the motion of the ship and they spent a lot of their time either in the toilets or showers heaving up the food they couldn't keep down. When you went down to the Mess Deck there were plenty of seconds if you felt like them.

We passed through the Straits of Gibraltar. Just a large lump of rock only valued for its strategic position. The Rock was on the left hand side and Morroco on the right for you land lubbers. The left side of a ship is Port the side you tie up to and the right hand side the Starboard for us nautical types. I loved leaning over the rails of the ship watching the porpoises racing us leaping the waves. The flying fish skipping from one wave to the next, an experience I would enjoy three more times.

The convoy kept loose formation with the Naval escort appearing now and again. The risk of attack was now negligible, North Africa having fallen to the Allies. We then appoached Port Said the entrance to the Suez Canal. We were to be one of the first convoy to go through the Canal after the Germans were out of North Africa. Previous to our convoys with the occupation of Egypt by the Germans and the Italians, all the convoys heading for the Far East had gone round South Africa. Where ships had been sunk in the Canal blocking it up, our engineers had dragged the wrecked hulks up the sides of the Canal so we could get through.

In Port Said the bum boats would pull up alongside the ship with their wares. The procedure would be to toss a rope up to us which was hauled aboard and on the end of the rope were different items - clothes and such like. They would shout out the prices and if they were lucky, they got their basket back minus the goodies. Sometimes the ships crew would put a hose on the bum boats nearly capsizing them. A good public relations exercise.

We laid anchor in the Bitter Lakes for the night. Very picturesque with the lights twinkling on the sides of the lake before carrying on to Port Suez. Again the bum boats bumming their wares with little success. They did allow one Egyptian aboard with a large suitcase. He opened it up and it had day old chicks in it. He put a couple on the deck and covered them with egg cups and when he lifted them the chicks had disappeared. Very entertaining. While we were cruising through the Med there was plenty of entertainment going on. Many of the draft were enlisted professional musicians including the aforementioned Tony Mercer who sang with the Signals Dance Band. They gave many shows to keep their hand in.

Tony was very popular with his rich Baritone voice singing the many ballads that came out prior, during and after the war. If the war did one thing it brought to the fore songwriters of the calibre of George Gershwin, Cole Porter, Jerome Kern, Sammy Kahn, Hoagy Carmichael and many more. Then of course you had all the American and also British Big Bands. Lyrics that made sense and melodies you could whistle (what happened to whistling?).

Another educational experience was a lecture given by a medical officer warning of the danger of sexually related diseases Gonorrhea and Syphilis. Technically known as a 'Knap hand'. He not only gave a verbal lecture, he had pickled penises in jars. Not a very pretty sight. The object was to deter you from visiting the brothels and free-lance prostitutes. I can tell you it certainly put me off. I kept my treasure in my pocket all the time I was in South East Asia Command. So we sailed through the Gulf of Suez with Jordan on the Port side and Egypt on the Starboard out into the Red Sea which wasn't Red at all. We often saw land on both sides consisting of desert and mountains. Arriving at the Port of Aden with some of the blackest people we had seen there were the usual bum boats and young boys diving for coins.

So into the Indian Ocean. Although there was a possibility of Japanese submarines about, the risk was negligible and the convoy of faster ships made a dash for their destination, ours being Bombay India. We disembarked, and straight onto a train heading for Mhow a Military Depot to the North of Bombay.

Chapter Six

'Arriving in South East Asia Command'

We still had our resident comedian with us in the shape of the elongated Lofty with more problems for him. He was never to let his rifle out of his sight, as if he lost it, that would be a Court Martial offence. There were many who would trade their life for a .303. Tribesmen from Afghanistan and Indian Independence on the horizon. So we were all a bit wary but not as wary as Lofty. He, never but never let go of his gun. It was on his back with the strap across the front of his body all the time.

When you travelled on an Indian train the carriage door would be opened inwards and somebody would be sitting on the top step enjoying the lovely scenery of which there is plenty in that country and of course the rushing air. The only problem is that by having the door opening inwards you blocked the toilet off that was in that corner. The toilet not one of those private ones you get in our railway carriages, but a porcelained hole in the floor of the speeding train and you crap onto the rushing rails beneath you.

So here we have our Lofty wanting to use the toilet. He would lower the window down, and with his rifle still on his back attempt to climb through the opening, being too shy to ask whoever was sitting on the step to let him through. Inevitably he would get stuck not being the most athletic of men. He in the toilet and his rifle jammed across the window on the outside. Eat your heart out Laurel and Hardy. We would have to plead with him to let his best friend off his shoulder and extricate him from the aperture. How did he manage to squat down with his rifle on his back? Remember there were no seats.

So we arrived at Mhow and were met by a Gurkha bagpipes band, they playing *'Scotland the Brave'* accompanying us to the barracks, two and three large plain buildings.

We had a rest and food and settled down for a well earned break after our train trip. I never saw Lofty anymore. He was probably sent to somewhere well out of the way in case he cocked the war up. The next day we went to visit the market an experience I never tired of. The aromas are the first thing that you realise, a large variety of spices and the Indian music creating and adding to the Eastern atmosphere. All sorts of wares to be bargained for. Bargaining is a way of life in the Indian markets and you are expected to haggle over anything you are, or indeed are not interested in. Stalls selling eats and drinks with the customers squatting on their haunches a favourite posture with them. Eating chapaties stuffed with green and red peppers. The hotter the better it seemed.

I remember picking up a Gurkha knife a Kukri. We had been told that if a Gurkha let you inspect his Kukri it had to draw blood. I drew this one from its leather sheaf and it cut through it giving my finger a nick. I didn't buy it.

The most popular form of transport was the tonga, a two wheeled vehicle drawn by a tonga Wallah on a bike. One of the first words you learn in India is 'wallah': Roughly meaning 'Fellah'. There are all sorts of wallahs. Dhobi (Laundry) the best known and most commonly used is Char Wallah. Wherever you find yourself in India the cry 'Char Wallah!' will assault your ears. The language we tried to master was Urdu, a Hindi language with some Persian words. Waste of time really as they spoke reasonable English whoever you spoke to.

After a short stay in Mhow we were kitted out with KD (Khaki Drill) and our pride and joy, a bush hat with one side turned up, with our Signals colours sewn on there. Several of us embarked on another train journey to a village by the Brahmaputra a large river that emptied into the Ganges which went to the Ganges Delta and into the Bay of Bengal.

So I arrived in Jorhat and joined up with the 56th Anti-Tank Regiment who had been pulled out for a well earned rest having fought at Imphal and Kohima. Very bloody battles where the Indian troops acquitted themselves with honour.

The journey from Mohw to Jorhat took several days through some breathtaking scenery. It was fascinating to see peacocks sunning themselves on the rock with their gorgeous tails spread out on display and the people in the paddy fields waving to the passing train. The windows of the carriages had to be wound up to stop pilfering. Not from humans, but tribes of monkeys or baboons that would ransack a carriage in minutes. They would attack you as well when the train was stationary.

We pulled into one station and there were these giant fruit bats (flying foxes) hanging from the surrounding trees. The engineer let off a blast from the train whistle and the whole colony took off practically shutting the sun out.

Stopping at the stations there were all the Wallahs selling their goods and some practising their professions. I was fascinated watching a dentist extracting a molar with no anaesthetic with a pair of pliers. Both patient and dentist squatting on all fours to perform this gut wrenching exercise.

Remember the porcelain toilets, just an elongated hole in the floor of the train? They weren't the most hygienic and if the train rolled which was often, it would upset your aim depositing excreta round the rim. Well these large cockroaches with hairy legs would be crawling around this second-hand food. They had Newcastle United coloured shirts on. The next time you saw them was when you took a loaf of bread from your big pack, and they would crawl out depositing anything their hairy legs had picked up. I won't apologise for relating the more unpleasant things that we experienced. I'm telling it how it was.

So I arrived at Jorhat and I seemed to be the only one joining the regiment. When we were placed in the Royal Corps of Signals we were told that we would go no further than Division HQ working forward to the regiments. Here was I being posted to the HQ of an Anti Tank Regiment. What was their armament?, - but three inch mortars with a range of two hundred yards. Here was I expecting to be swanning back at a Divisional HQ tapping out morse miles away from the action and where had I finished up? Two hundred bloody yards from the enemy.

I was the youngest soldier in the regiment, later to be given the name of 'Chico' meaning Boy in Urdu. The war-weary Gunners in Regimental HQ adopted me like big brothers. I will remember Jorhat for one thing - being turned inside out.

One day I went to the 'bog' thirty two times. I cannot call this evil smelling latrine a toilet, you went down this rough path to this bamboo shack. In case you haven't caught on I had the 'RUNS' and I went thirty-two times in one day. The bog was just two planks laid parallel and you squatted over the gap like a dog. The pit was alive with every scavenging crawly you can imagine and more, all inspecting your anus. After sitting over this obnoxious pit thirty two times you felt like I've already said, that you had been turned inside out.

I went to see the medical officer and he assured me I hadn't got dysentery, just a cold in the stomach. He gave me some jollop to dry it up and advised me to sleep with a towel across my middle. I was perched over the pit one day and a Brummie asked me *'Where you from son?'. 'London'. 'Where abouts?'. 'Walthamstow mate'*. He informed me there was a clerk in HQ from there name of Nat Horwitz. I couldn't believe it.

When we used to go to the Youth Club in Walthamstow there was this Jewish lad Nat Horwitz, a fellow who oozed charm and personality. Everything he did he was good at. His top achievement was ballroom dancing, he was a very good amateur. Although Jewish, his looks were Latin. He had a dark complexion with black hair, a thin moustache ala Rudolph Valentino the old silent film actor. A full set of flashing white pearly teeth and the personality to go with it as well as the chat with the opposite sex. When there was a dance at the club Nat took the floor with an equally vivacious partner either doing the quick step or the dance that he excelled at which matched his looks and style, the tango. Everyone would clear the floor for them to give a wonderful exhibition of this most sensuous and rhythmical dance.

Here he was with 56th Anti Tank. We didn't know one another at all really from the club. Me being just one of a gang of boys and him being a star so to speak. I located him in one of the tents playing bridge. (What else?) and I introduced myself. Obviously my encounter at the pit had told him of my existence. He probably didn't recognise me, but that wasn't Nat's style. He made me feel like he did. I found over a period he was probably the best liked gunner at HQ. He always had time for anyone. I didn't see much of him during the campaign, but plenty when we got back to India.

Another memory of Jorhat was dyeing our khaki drill issue. We weren't issued with camouflage clothing but they had this large drum of green gunge boiling away merrily. We had to get a long broom handle and put all of our clothing in. It actually worked very well on the light brown kits as the dye didn't get into the folds of the clothes so that when they came out they were green and brown stripes. There was something they had overlooked which I'll come to later.

We were just a small Royal Corps of Signals unit with the regiment with a full Corporal whose name I can't remember, a pipe smoking L/Cpl Charlie Elliot from Ilford; a bespectacled gentleman in his person and manner; a man who carried his bible everywhere; a man I respected all the time I was with him. Charlie was a Scout Master in civvy street. The full Cpl; L/Cpl, and myself fully trained wireless operators. Then there was Alf Palmer again from Ilford. He was the boffin trained as a wireless mechanic. The other member of our Signal unit was our fifteen cwt truck driver who kept himself very much to himself.

Charlie and I were the personal wireless operators to our C/O the Honourable David Balfour, son of a Scottish Laird, Lord Kinross. He didn't join the regiment until we joined the 5th Indian Division later. The three of us were driven by a Scotsman John known as 'Jock'. I wonder why? Jock took it upon himself that being an old sweat he would take me under his wing. Be my guardian angel. Some hopes. No way José.

While looking in the fifteen cwt I found a Sten gun. An all metal cheap repeater meant for close quarter combat, but by all reports it had killed more of our own troops than the enemy. So it was not to be trusted as I was to find out. I took it back to our tent, cleaned and oiled it then off to the firing range. I had found some ammunition and put a clip on the gun. I pointed it up the range and rat-a-tat-tat the whole magazine went off there was no way of controlling it. I began to realise why it had been thrown in the back of the lorry. In other words it was dangerous being faulty. I hoped it wouldn't malfunction the next time I used it. Wishful thinking.

Chapter Seven

'The Road to Burma'

So the regiment formed up in convoy to start the long trek over the Naga Hills which were about four thousand feet up then down into Burma.

Our acting CO was a Major McTurk. A gent who had been in Burma too long and 'was a bit gun happy'. He had his gun holster slung low like one of those old Western gunslingers on the frontiers. The trip took us several days. We passed Imphal and Kohima that saw some bloody fighting. Alf had just joined the regiment then so you can imagine what a baptism that was for him.

The Japanese were hoping to cross the Indian frontier and the whole of that continent would have been at their mercy. The British, Indian and Commonwealth joint armies held firm and the Japanese retreated back down into Burma. So we started out on this tough trip on a fairly flat terrain, but which the road was 'not'. It was fairly wide but had traffic calming great dips and humps. It was just a dust road covered in what seemed to be red brick dust which penetrated every crevice and orifice in your body. The springs of our vehicles were very truly tested and we had to cover our faces with anything to stop choking, leaving just a gap for your eyes. We stopped by a wide river and everyone dived in leaving a red scum on top of the water. We then continued and if a gap opened up between you and the vehicle in front, a jeep would come bouncing up. *'Close up there!'* would be the command.

There were bandits in this area and they would raid a convoy for food and arms. It was all jungle each side of this track and you could see where the Japs had been living in very rough conditions. The shelters where they slept were two forked sticks in the ground with a length of bamboo across them and covered in jungle foliage. They had kipped down like this for two years. No wonder they gained the reputation of being the best jungle fighters.

When we stopped to relieve ourselves the convoy would close up and we'd all jump out each side of our vehicle to repel the bandits if they attacked. We stopped once and this big old

In convoy on the red dusty road.

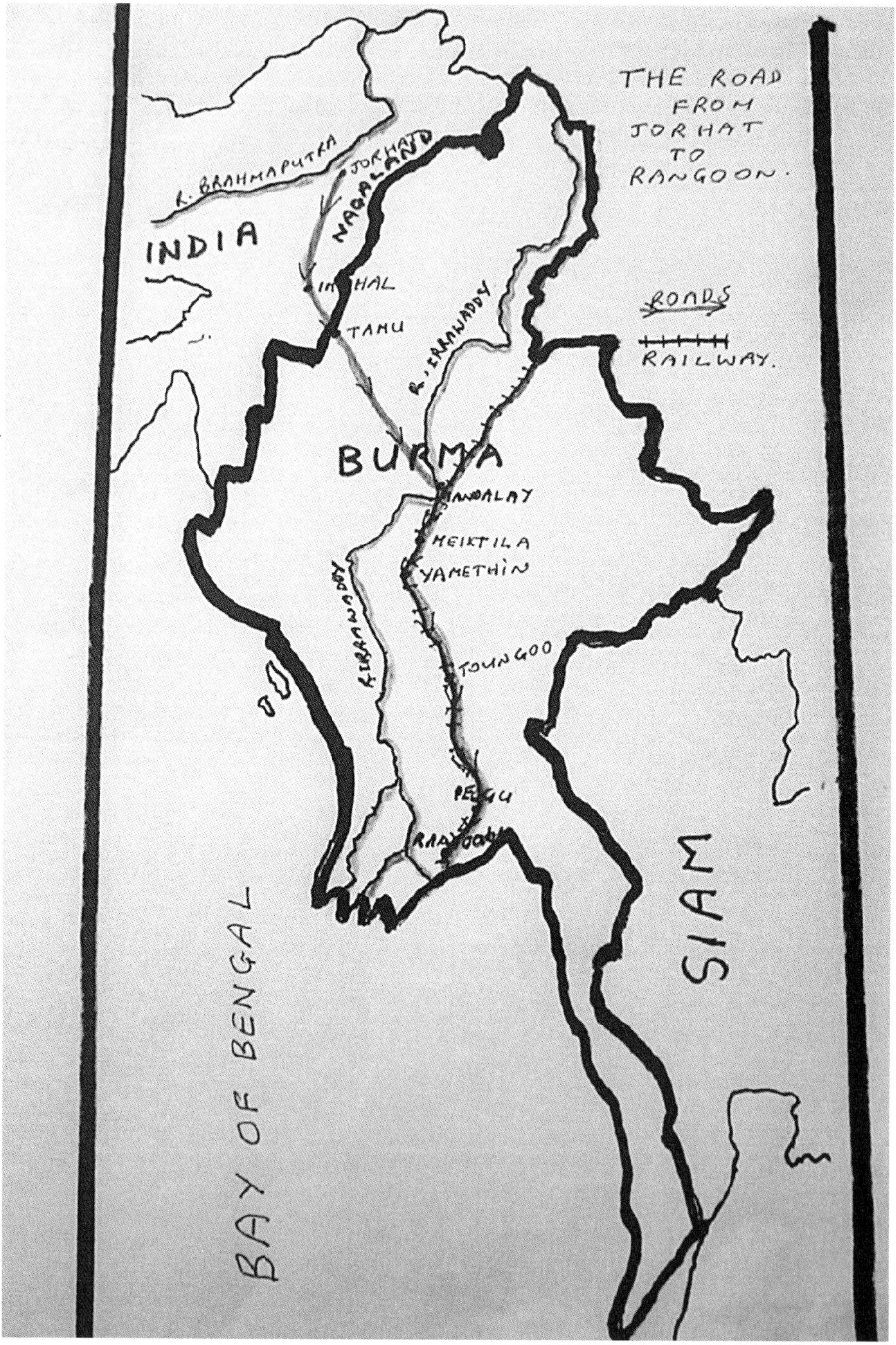

The Road from Jorhat to Rangoon.

hare came lolloping out of the jungle. This was an opportunity for Major 'Wyatt' McTurk to show off his prowess with his six shooter. He drew his pistol took careful aim at this innocent hare just munching away merrily. The Major unloaded all six bullets at 'Bugs Bunny' who carried on chewing with the bullets flying harmlessly past him. He gave the gunfighter a thud on the ground with his back legs and lolloped back into the jungle none the worse for wear. I did have my Sten at the ready just in case.

A little further up the road it was my turn to make a prat of myself. We had stopped again and I thought maybe I should check the safety on the Sten. A mistake, as soon as I took it off, the whole bloody magazine went off again. Wyatt drew from the hip and the rest of the battle-weary gunners hit the deck thinking we were being attacked. Major McTurk looked round for the guilty culprit and with my gun still smoking he hollered *'Who gave that bloody fool a Sten. Where did you get it from soldier?'*

'I found it in the back of the fifteen hundred weight Sir!' 'Well put it back there and equip yourself with a rifle'. My thoughts were 'What about you, and that harmless hare'.

We now started climbing up into the Naga Hills home of the Naga Hill Tribesmen to probably four thousand feet up a long winding road that snaked round the 'mountain' side (Come on they are four thousand feet up. Surely more than just hills.) Again just a dirt road meant for bullock carts and the hill tribes to walk on. The top surface if you could call it that, just loose soil with the cant leaning towards the outside. If a vehicle slid over there was a nasty drop with no means of recovery.

Initially we didn't see the Nagas then they started to appear. Fierce looking little men with a ready grin. We were warned they could easily be moved to violence. We were also told they were intelligent people with a sense of humour. Their ancestors had been headhunters and in their villages of bamboo huts built on stilts, of which we saw none, they still displayed on sharpened sticks shrunken heads. They were pro-British and were part of the resistance that had prevented the Japanese from invading India.

They were and are, very protective of their women and hated the Japs who had violated them during their advance on Kohima. They had collected info on the Japanese movements and were our allies who guided our columns and carried our supplies. They also brought in our wounded under heavy fire. Many of the British troops owed their lives to the 'Great little gentlemen of the jungle' as one writer called them.

To them the human head is the seat of wisdom and the human soul. He who owned another's head gained prosperity in this world and the admiration of his fellow man. Also a guaranteed happiness in the after world. A boy would not become a man until he had taken another's head.

Their central purpose of life was the quest for heads. With the Christian missionaries head hunting had died out but I wouldn't mind betting there were a few Japanese heads around the Naga villages.

This diary of memoirs are just from my memory with no written notes. This can be fallible as we all know, but I seem to recall the Nagas had a two handed sword that slid into a bamboo scabbard. I also seem to remember that they had elephant hide bound round their calves.

Chapter Eight

'The Stench of Death'

We descended from the Naga Hills to a place named Tamu. The place was deserted as the people had scarpered with the Japanese withdrawing and us advancing. We crossed a large river the Irrawaddy where our engineers had erected a Bailey Bridge across. It was a bit hairy driving our vehicles across this floating engineering feat. It took me back to when I was on war work before being called up. One of the projects I was working on was the end posts for these bridges. They were very heavy welded fabrications of one inch plate. We would jig them up to be welded together. The weight as you can imagine was very heavy. Did I help to make the end posts on this bridge we were crossing?

We entered a town named Miektila. Charlie Elliott and myself were in the CO's jeep. The CO Colonel Balfour hadn't joined us yet. Our driver was Jock who had seen it all. The town boasted an air strip and you entered it probably along the strip when this overpowering nauseating smell assaulted your nostrils. I asked Jock what this sweet sickening stench was. His reply was *'You'll see soon enough son'*.

On each side of the road the Japanese had dug trenches and from them hung the bloated bodies of dead Japs. In time the gases in their stomachs would swell and explode their entrails.I would see this many times with horses and bullocks. The enemy would also leave the odd dead body either human or animal down a village well to contaminate it.

Every bridge would be manned by suicide squads and they would be laying there bloated or exploded with this stench of death that I had queried as we entered Meiktila. There was a large lake there that we camped by and we were told not to bathe in the lake or drink from it. With dead bodies being washed up we didn't need warning, the Japanese contaminated all water supplies. Our drinking and washing water was from a water wagon. It was a large round tank mounted on the chassis of a lorry which often got stuck in the mud with the water slopping about in the tank. They shovelled literally pounds of chlorine into the tank and it looked like milk when you drew some out. So thick you could chew it and it tasted like chalk, but it did kill the bacteria.

The Japanese had occupied the town for about two years and had made themselves as comfortable as possible. They had dug quite substantial bunkers into the ground and lined them with shiny plated tin. There was one that the Sherman tanks had blown up and there were limbs protruding from the debris in every direction. A jeep full of Americans turned up looking for souvenirs which they probably flogged in Calcutta or back home in the States. They spotted a Japanese officer's two-handed sword protruding from under the rotting bodies and they got a plank from somewhere and levered the bloated bodies apart so they could capture the sword. You can imagine the stench and swarms of flies that came up.

Chapter Nine

'The Final Push'

I've read several accounts of the Burma campaign mainly about the years before I arrived to add my weight to the battle. With Imphal, Kohima and other bloody battles being well documentated. The last six months when we took the rail and road link from Miektila doesn't get much of a mention as the Japanese were in disarray. It was a job that had to be done to complete the capture of Burma. This is my own personal account of the battle, just a young soldier's experiences of it.

I have read of the Chindits named after the stone tigers that guard the temples in Burma. They were a band of trained jungle warfare soldiers commanded by General Orde Wingate. They were dropped behind enemy lines using guerrilla tactics. They were ably supported by the Gurkhas and would attack in small groups.

The operation lasted three months and just 2200 of the 3000 sent in returned, many of them not considered fit for further operations. The morale of the British troops had been low and the exploits of Wingate's Chindits did much to restore the morale of the Allied Forces, knowing that the previously undefeated invincible Japanese Army could be beaten.

Orde Wingate died in an air crash before the end of the war. South East Asia Command had now been taken over by Lord Louis Mountbatten and the 14th Army by Sir William Slim known to his troops as Bill Slim. Lord Mountbatten's influence succeeded in getting much needed air support including transport aircraft. Supply by air then became the norm for forward troops.

The spirit of the 14th Army became stronger under General Bill Slim's command, with forward units being encouraged to sit tight instead of dispersing as they had been.

In our drive down to Rangoon (Now known as Yangon) we would be supplied by air drop from Dakotas as we would be travelling too fast for supply vehicles to keep up with us. (Dakota an American transport plane). Two Divisions would be used to capture the road and railway down to Rangoon.

If you study the map, the road and rail link from Yamethin to Rangoon run parallel down the length of this very narrow country and once you capture them you have the life line of Burma. Our regiment the 56th Anti Tank had now joined the 5th Indian Division and we in turn now had our CO who had flown in. When we first got in the jeep with Colonel David Balfour he turned his head and asked Jock to introduce him to his two wireless operators. It was L/Cpl Elliot first and then he turned the other way to confront me. *'This is Signalman Dudley Sir!'.'How old are you son?'. 'Nineteen Sir!'. 'Why you're just a baby. I shall call you Chico'.* Meaning 'Boy' in Urdu and it stuck.

A Douglas Dakota, the first of over 1900 Dakotas received by the RAF arrived in India in 1942. Dakotas served in every theatre of the war, notably in Burma, during the D-Day landings and the airborne assault on Arnhem in 1944.

The battle plan was for two divisions to leap frog down the road. The one division to take say twenty miles and the other to pass through the forward division and take another stretch of road and rail. The other division being the British 19th Division.

The Japanese isolated on the east of the country had nowhere to go except the ocean, or cross the road and rail link to get into Siam (Now Thailand). There was one criteria, the monsoon season was now upon us. A monsoon if you haven't experienced one is practically impossible to describe. One instance a dried up river bed can become a raging torrent. Our vehicles were four wheel drive but with tanks and half tracks if they did get stuck they could be towed out.

I think it was the imminence of the monsoons that convinced Lord Louis to push on (after consulting me). The Japs were not expecting it. The two divisions were made up of British and Indian infantry with artillery and Sherman tanks. Burma is mainly jungle with large teak trees looming over you and we saw practically nothing of the Burmese. They took off into the jungle.

Plenty of snakes, scorpions, poisonous insects of every description. The most lethal I suppose was the female mosquito, giving you malaria which can prove fatal. You were given Mepachrine tablets which after a while turned your skin yellow. Handy if you met an oriental gentleman who would mistake you for one of his.

Didn't see any big cats or indeed elephants of which Burma is famous for. After travelling through the day we would stretch the tarpaulin from the fifteen cwt. dig a hole for your hip to fit into and get your head down. The monsoon was just starting and the hole would be full of water in the morning. At night the noise of the other Division's tanks would be heard passing through our Division. As previously stated we were on air-drop from Dakota transport planes and our food mainly being 'K' Ration. This was an oblong box which when you opened it contained another, covered in a hard candle grease substance to preserve the contents.

The contents consisted of all sorts of goodies whichever meal it was. There was a Spam like meat, cheese like a bar of soap, cardboard biscuits and cigarettes of the Camel brand that tasted more like camel excrement than tobacco. A product of America but thankfully at some times we were glad of them. The transporter planes would drop their contents willy-nilly on any clear area and often the natives would get there first and help themselves. Couldn't really blame them after the Japanese occupation.

A little story of what happened when we reached a town named Toungoo. It was pitch black and we were stuck on the outskirts of the town waiting to cross a bridge which I'm sure was another Bailey. I had been travelling with the Colonel in the Jeep, we had dismounted and if I remember correctly, we were being shelled by a lone Japanese artillery gun. I was lying across the bonnet of the vehicle and could vaguely see another figure there. The figure was the Colonel who enquired *'Who's that?' 'Chico Sir!'*. I had my .303 cocked to repel the enemy. *'Get back into the Jeep Chico I've heard about you, and guns'*. He was due for repatriation and didn't want to be shot on the last knockings by one of his own men. Bet he would have soon called for me if we had been attacked.

As we passed through Toungoo we found we could not transmit or receive wireless signals from in the town itself. To lock onto a frequency with another wireless set, you both tune into the same frequency and then net in. The other set will send the signal out and you have this small knob which you rotate as you receive the high pitched signal until it descends into a low pitch and you are now netted into the other set.

We tried this by getting two sets that were mounted on jeeps but as we moved away the signal just vanished.

So where is this leading to? When we returned to Toungoo after Rangoon was taken, we still encountered the same problem but heard that some Sikh signallers were working just outside the town to Rangoon some distance away. So we (that is Charlie Elliot, a driver and myself) went looking for these signallers and found them on the outskirts of Toungoo with just a length of telephone wire hanging from a tree signalling to Rangoon.

We decided to try ourselves and found a suitable tree to hang our length of wire from. Someone had to shin up the tree with the wire. Now I noticed that there were tell tale little clay tunnels going up the trunk which told me that the tree was occupied by red ants - nasty little bastards that will attack in numbers if disturbed.

This is where Charlie the ex-scoutmaster's scouting experience came to the fore. Now Charlie wasn't really built for shinning up trees being on the heavy side, but he was not to be deterred and he started clambering up the trunk. He fell to the ground screaming in agony with loads of the ants clinging to his flesh. The ants inject acid when they attack and when you try to pull them off the head is left hanging on. Charlie was left with many small red weals all over the upper part of his body. I suppose I should have told him about those tell-tale clay tunnels.

It was because of this problem we had with no reception in Toungoo, that when we came back to the town I was sent to man a wireless set on the outskirts on the bridge.

At about the time I received a message from Division HQ about 2,000 Japanese troops just down the road that I stumbled on a station relaying the celebrations from Trafalgar Square for the victory in Europe. It wasn't too long before they dropped the bombs on Hiroshima and Nagasaki and the Japanese surrendered unconditionally in Rangoon on May 3rd 1945 to Lord Louis Mountbatten and Sir William (Bill) Slim.

Another dodgy morning we had formed into a box for the night. This is a procedure when you bed down for the night. The two inch mortars are zeroed in to fire cross-fire and theoretically this will catch any enemy attacking of getting too close, being caught in the cross-fire. At daybreak the vehicles would disperse in case of air attack which was getting less of a threat everyday as we were approaching Rangoon air-strip. We were probably a couple of hundred miles from there, lined up for our breakfast at the back of the Cook's three tonner.

At dawn American Mustang fighter planes would appear to cover any threat from the air. They had square tips to their wings making them very discernable. Trouble was the Japanese Zero fighters had the same shaped wings, but one of them did have its rudder cut square as well, I can't remember which. So there we were lining up for our nosh when this fighter plane came zooming over us, we just casually looking up. Then someone shouted 'Zero!!'. It dropped one anti personnel bomb and we had flattened on the ground. The bloody thing landed by my head but didn't explode.

Guess what? and you won't believe this, but it's absolutely true. We were still observing Summer Time and someone somewhere hadn't altered their clocks the one hour. I would think it was the Americans. Only do they alter their clocks?

The Zero was shot down by Anti-Aircraft guns, the pilot a woman unhurt. Earlier on we came to a village which I believe was Yamethin and the tanks moved in and reported it clear of Japs. The infantry followed and the Nips were still dug in. So they called for an air strike which reminded me of that Sunday morning in Walthamstow when Hurricanes and Spitfires came low over the house tops. This time it was Mosquitos. Not the insects, but a new Fighter Bomber they had started using in Burma. They smashed this village to the ground. Any Japs our infantry found there were either dead or wounded.

So the capture of the road and rail link down to Rangoon continued. We got 60 miles North of Rangoon to a town by the name of Pegu. Then the news came through that the marines had landed and taken Rangoon beating us to it. We were issued with tents to pitch and get our clothes and ourselves dried out.

They were tents that accommodated four people. We had just got ours erected and pegged down when I was told the Colonel wanted a word with me. I was still wet and cold when I found him by the Jeep with Jock his driver. The Colonel spoke *'Chico we're going down to Rangoon to have a look and I was wondering if you would like to come with us'*. I declined the offer explaining I wanted to get dried out.

Now in the great plan for the capture of the road and rail link down to the city, everything had been planned meticulously but they hadn't taken into account one phenomenon. They say sliced bread was one of the greatest inventions but I would personally go for the zip, especially the non-metal type. The phenomenon the Commanders hadn't taken into account was the action of water on metal. I don't know the chemical formula, but it's known as rust and all our uniforms had metal buttons which meant by the time we had reached Pegu, we had no buttons on our uniforms including our flies. So there was I in front our Commanding Officer being dismissed. I turned on my heel after throwing him up one and he halted me in my tracks. *'Chico! before you go'*. *'Yes Sir!'*. *'Put that thing away'*. To my extreme embarrassment when I looked downwards in the direction the Colonel and Jock were looking, my winkle was poking out from my shorts doing its impersonation of a little bit of boiled pork. I must confess for one who seems to attract humourous and embarrassing situations this was my worst or best. Take your pick.

We didn't stop too long at Pegu and were sent back inland to where else but Toungoo. It wasn't only our regiment, but Indian troops as well. We set up homes in the huts on stilts, never seeing the Burmese at all.

Chapter Ten

'John L Sullivan and his demise'

When we travelled in convoy, lots of the vehicles would have chickens tied by one leg on the backs of them as means of eggs and at times a change in our diet. When we got settled into our bamboo huts we tied our camouflage nets around the stilts supporting the huts and we had a chicken run. We also clipped the birds wings so they couldn't fly over the netting.

One morning we had an extra chicken in our run, but it was a cockerel. A dapper little jungle fowl looking like our Bantams back home with glorious feathering and a gorgeous iridescent flowing tail. He had been having his way with our hens and also ate their food which was mainly dried bread. At night he had it away over the top of the netting and went to roost in the jungle. He would be back in his harem the next morning. He also had very long spurs like a Fighting Cock.

Now we had heard that the Indian troops kept fighting cocks that they put against each other's with wagers on the outcome. So we wandered across to their lines to have a look at these gladiators. They showed us their Champion which was a large cross Rhode Island Red. A real nasty looking bit of work. His blood red comb looking like a rugby union player's cauliflower 'ear'ole. We challenged them to fight our cock with a wager on the outcome.

We had managed to catch 'John L Sullivan' as we decided to call our little warrior. We had fixed the netting so he couldn't get out and one brave lad caught him and put him in a box ready for his first professional fight the next day. Actually he wasn't all that wild now, as he had got used to us feeding him and we were also providing him with a lot of 'nooky'.We went across to the Indian lines and they had an empty hut at ground level where they organised the fights. There was their Champion strutting about looking for his next victim.

We let John L out of the box and he spotted his antagonist straight away. He was over and on the other chicken's back before you could say John L. Now we hadn't realised, but all that treading of our hens was the best training he could have had. He grabbed the other cockerel's comb and wouldn't let go, raking its back with his long fighting spurs. The Indian trainers of the big Rhode Island Cock called *'Enough!'* Their Champion no longer could be called that, as John L had taken his title. I am not a lover of Blood Sports and never went to watch our little tearaway in another fight of which he had another five before tragedy struck. He did win all his fights convincingly. He was left with his wives as he had now become a valuable bird to his team of trainers and they didn't want him sloping off into the jungle to be eaten by predators, but he had gone AWOL.

It was now in late April of 1945 and the regiment was getting ready for repatriation, so the Sergeants Mess decided to kill all their chickens. So let me introduce you to the Sergeants Mess Cook who was also a butcher by trade. A large blond man hailing from Birmingham. He had killed all their birds. We still hadn't seen our champion John L Sullivan, then we realised what must have happened. Our randy little jungle fowl with his insatiable sexual appetite must have got in with the Sergeants hens and met his match in the big blond cook. The only consolation to us, not John L, was that one of our group had watched the cook going about the business of dispatching the birds and he said it was a revelation.

The big man just went amongst the fowl placing his middle finger and index finger each side of the birds neck bringing them up to the victims jaws. He then lifted them off the floor and with a quick jerk the poor unfortunates were left twitching on the deck. All very humane and nice to know if that was our cock's demise it was quick. So our champion's record read like this. Number of fights 7. Won 6. Lost 1 to a 16st blond heavyweight giving away 222lbs. Should have called him Jimmy Wilde.

Chapter Eleven

'Snakes and Butterflies'

I was then sent to man a wireless set on the town side of the bridge at Toungoo which at one time a few hundred years ago was the capital of Burma. We had a Captain, Sergeant and about twenty of us other ranks and the wireless was in touch with Division HQ passing messages to our Regimental HQ. We spent our time playing cards and smoking 'Players' cigarettes and scoffing ourselves with tinned milk and tinned fruit. The Players fags we were lucky to get hold of because of the natives reaching them before we could. The next time we saw our smokes was in Rangoon being sold back to us.

Our Sergeant was a most interesting man who had worked as a Game Warden in Kenya. Sgt. Coulter was an expert on most animals especially snakes. He had made himself a large net to catch these magnificent butterflies. Some were quite large as big as the spread of your hand and they fluttered around in the jungle behind the fairly large house on stilts that we were occupying. The Sgt. would mount them on a card by pinning them through the thorax. Sealing them in the cellophane from our cigarette packets and surround the bodies with camphor to preserve them which he had with him obviously being prepared for collecting the butterflies. I often borrowed the net as he encouraged me in my interest in animals in general.

Our latrine was about twenty yards behind the house with a rough path to it. I would take the net with me and sometimes catch a butterfly. One day

I was making my way to the 'bog', as it was still only two planks over a pit, but it had lime in it when I was halted in my tracks by what I thought was a large reptile across the path. The Sergeant had told us that if we were confronted by a snake, to shake the net at it to get it to strike and leg it back to the house. I reported back to the Sgt. who went to investigate. It was the shed skin of a Hooded King Cobra not the snake itself.

The latrine was put out of bounds and we had to take a shovel with us to do our business nearer the house accompanied by another soldier. He explained that most snakes would retreat if they heard you approaching, but not a male King Cobra which as it had shed its skin was rampant and looking for a mate. It would actually lie in ambush. I could picture it. You perched over the pit and the King Cobra is looking for a mate and mistakes your pride and joy for a Hooded female giving it a lovebite.

Sgt. Coulter brought a Russell's Viper in one evening. Not a large snake but very venomous. He had it gripped on its neck opening its mouth to expose two very long fangs. He had stretched a piece of cloth over a jar and milked the venom from the reptile. Very educational. He also captured a Banded Krait to demonstrate the same procedure. The snake was banded black and yellow.

Chapter Twelve
'Trophy Hunting'

Now most of my comrades had trophies to take home including the blond Sgt. Cook. He showed me a collection of beautiful rubies tied up in a handkerchief, Burma being one of the biggest sources of this precious stone. The Sergeant had the best means of getting hold of them, trading large tins of corned beef for the rubies which he told me he would get mounted when he got home for his wife. They were worth a fortune.

Here was I with nothing. I never saw anyone with a Samurai Sword the best prize you could wish for. However there was one memento that some of them had which had been fairly easy to come by. All the Japanese soldiers were given a flag of their country, this being a large red Rising Sun on a white background. They would roll them up and carry them in their steel helmets. So if you spotted a Jap bloated body and no-one had got there before you, there was a fair chance you would find a beautiful silk flag to take home. So how was I going to get hold of one of these trophies?

Toungoo itself was strictly out of bounds as there were still plenty of isolated Japs about. Did this worry Chico? No way. I have often recalled what I did all those years ago, I wasn't brave but bloody stupid. Being young you don't envisage anything happening to yourself. So I armed myself with my .303 and slid out of the house into the town. Not large concrete buildings just bamboo huts on stilts, but not all I found out. Some with just a gap of probably a couple of feet off the ground for the monsoons. I rummaged around through some of them and found nothing. Then bingo! in one I found some photos of Japanese soldiers and a leather ammunition pouch.

Four Japanese soldiers photograph found Toungoo, Burma 1945.

Also a photo of two little Japanese children in black velvet suits with frilly lace collars, making me realise that although we despised them for what they had done when rampaging through the Far East, they still had families at home.

Still nothing worth boasting about. Then I found a flag which if I remember was under a dirty sheet on a charpoy (bed). It wasn't silk, but a tatty old cotton one with Japanese writing over it. I managed to creep back into our house with no-one realising I had been AWOL. Probably some of the other ranks may have thought I was catching butterflies as I had taken the net with me to make them think that. So here was I with the leather ammunition pouch, some photos and my tatty cotton flag which I still have now.

Two Japanese children. Photograph found Toungoo, Burma 1945.

Japanese soldier photograph found Toungoo, Burma 1945.

Japanese soldier photograph found Toungoo, Burma 1945.

I was wondering if someone would swap my flag for a silk one and I showed it to some of my comrades. They told me I had something far more valuable than a common silk flag which were fairly easy to come by, but a regimental flag with battle honours on it (though I was more recently and reliably informed that it wasn't actually a regimental one, but the sort given to a soldier by his family to remind him of home). The writing is a bit more faded now as when I brought it home my wife gave it a wash, but I still have my tatty family flag.

I was on the wireless set one night when a message came through from Divisional HQ in five letter code which I didn't have. I took it to the captain and he phoned Regimental HQ. The message was to tell us that there were two thousand Japanese troops two hundred yards down the road on the other side of the bridge with hardly any guns or ammo. They were in dire straits with all sorts of illness and believe it or not some comfort girls with them. These would be Burmese girls they had captured and forced into prostitution.

We were told to sit tight and let them cross the road on their way to Siam. The message was passed round the house and you could hear the gunners putting a .303 bullet up the spout of their rifles and laying there listening for the enemy. Thankfully they didn't show up.

They must have reached our infantry the next day as you could hear small arms fire and the unmistakable sound of Bren guns. I leave it to your imagination. I wouldn't think many of the two thousand reached Siam.

The regiment was then told to pack all our gear and form up in convoy to go down the road to Rangoon in preparation for the return to India on the first leg back home for re-patriation.The Japanese accepted unconditional surrender on May 3rd 1945. We arrived in Rangoon and were billeted in a large green building that had housed an American Bank before the country's occupation by the Japanese. It was several storeys high and we were on the second floor. HQ that is. The building was on the waterfront and the Japs had really turned it over. All the safes had been blown and the floors were in a hell of a state.

Chapter Thirteen

'Rangoon and the Shwedagon Pagoda'

The next day several of us went to have a look at the city and the Japanese had left it in a mess with grass growing up in the main streets, yet we were amazed to find a Chinese Restaurant open.

We had heard about the Shwedagon Pagoda which we decided to visit, this being one of the Ancient Wonders of the Old World. As you approach a Burmese village you will hear this pleasant tinkling of bells coming from the tops of the pagodas. As we have chapels and churches in our villages, they have their pagodas. Shrines to Buddha's their God and their place of worship.

The Shwedagon is the greatest pagoda of its kind in the world 'Shwe' means 'Gold' and Dagon is the former name of Yangon (the ancient name of Rangoon which it has reverted back to). Hence the Swedagon which means the golden pagoda at the city of Dagon (Rangoon). It is believed to have been built 2,600 years ago during Buddha's lifetime.

Shwedagon Pagoda, Rangoon.

We arrived at the pagoda and were told by the monks to remove our shoes and socks as you are only allowed to enter bare footed. The pagoda has a height of three hundred and twenty six feet and is one thousand four hundred and twenty feet in circumference at the base. We had to climb hundreds of steps to get to the top of this unique place of worship. The main pagoda was surrounded by hundreds of small Buddha's guarded by iron railings that had been broken into. The Buddha's had been decorated by precious stones in their foreheads, but they had been prized out and stolen - all sitting cross legged. It was a once in a lifetime experience that I wish could remember more of. It is now back to its former glory, the top being covered by large sheets of gold leaf which you will see from miles away when you leave the port of Rangoon.

So back to our billet in the Yankee bank and another embarrassing moment for Chico. During our trip down through Burma I had often seen this Sergeant, always he seemed to be swigging from a bottle of whisky. Where his supply came from who knows. He was member of HQ and a true alcoholic (technically known as a 'piss artist' extrordinaire. A member of the bar.)

It was to be our last night in Rangoon. We were due to embark on a freighter next morning for Calcutta. L/Cpl Charlie Elliot, Alf Palmer and I had kept low. So we would be embarking for Calcutta with the rest of the

56th who were due for Blighty bound and we would be transferred before they set sail for home. Everyone was drinking heavily although the next morning, the 56th Anti Tank Regiment were to march through the city with the Colonel Rt. Hon. David Balfour leading his men to the fore of the regiment. Regimental flag unfolded.

This 'Alchi' Sergeant wandered over to me with his bottle of the hard stuff. *'Get your mug Chico and have a proper drink'*. I held my pint mug out and he said *'Say when!'* .The golden liquid gurgled into my mug until it was brimful and I cried out *'When!'*. Now I cannot remember ever drinking whisky before but I'd show these old soldiers, so I put it down the hatch in one draft.

Our washing facility was a half biscuit tin with a rope through a hole each side and a short length of bamboo for a handle. It was used for washing and shaving, but I found another use for it. I had my head stuck in it all night vomiting and retching. I wanted to die. I never ever thought anyone could feel like that and I was to form up with the rest of the regiment in the morning. The next morning my mates got me cleaned up and packed my equipment. They even emptied my half biscuit tin and washed it out. We fell in outside the bank and I was put between two big men who held me up. 'Left-turn!' came the order and I found myself with no support. I wasn't too steady on my plates of meat (feet) but after emptying the contents of my stomach all night into the half biscuit tin, my mind was fairly clear.

So the 56th anti-tank regiment marched off with me staggering in the rear through Rangoon with the Colonel proudly leading his men and the regimental flag waving proudly in the fore with the citizens being suitably impressed. I was having a job keeping up, but concentrated with my eyes fixed solidly on the last ranks in front of me. I had my rifle slung across my shoulders and my half biscuit tin hanging on one of the straps on my big pack. It was rattling away which, if I had been in step, would have been to the rhythm of marching feet, but with my staggering it must have sounded like a cha-cha-cha.

If someone had called out 'About turn' I would have been at the front of the Regiment probably with my Japanese flag tied to my rifle waving proudly and the Rt. Hon. would have been wondering *'Where the bloody hell is my Regiment'*. So we arrived at the docks and after a while I got there. They were loading a landing craft with kit bags. I had slumped down on top of them.

Captain 'Chalky' White was in charge of the loading and someone enquired *'What shall we do with him Sir!?'* meaning me. *'Throw him on with the kitbags'* came the reply and that's how I left Rangoon laying on top of some kitbags on a landing craft feeling rough, but pleased I had made it. The freighter we journeyed across the Bay of Bengal was a bit basic with a rope stretched along the top deck separating the British troops from the Indian. Funny they didn't do that when we were fighting the Japs together. I kept strictly to a couple of beers.

The journey took us across where that terrible Tsunami destroyed so much of the region and took so many innocent lives sixty years on. As we left Rangoon I remember looking back at the Shwedagon Pagoda with its gold pinnacle glistening in the sun. Even in my hazy state a wonderful memory.

Chapter Fourteen

'Return to India'

We docked in Calcutta and were loaded onto lorries and taken out to Dum-Dum just outside the city. Any serviceman who has been to Calcutta knows Dum-Dum Camp.

My memories of Calcutta are a bit vague but remember Nat Horwitz? We got together and I remember our jeep driver warning me of all the iniquities of Calcutta. Poor old Jock, he meant well for the safety of a young inexperienced soldier and I thank him for it. Exuberance of youth John. So Nat and I jumped on a 15cwt to taste what Calcutta had to offer. We found ourselves in a Record shop playing some jazz records and got to chat with two young 2nd Lieutenants who were also into jazz. The outcome was Nat and I arranged to meet them in a club that evening.

Nat and I began to get to know each other better talking about Walthamstow and the Youth Club. We got dressed up and met these two officers as arranged in this night club in Calcutta. There was an area for dancing but we sat on an elevated area at a table for four chatting and drinking. The evening was going well, talking about jazz which I had been listening to since I left school and am still doing so today. Then our new friends started buying rounds of short whisky. Nat and I couldn't afford this on our pay but it didn't seem to worry them unduly.

After my experience in Rangoon I suppose I should have known better, but probably thought I could handle shorts (as long as they had buttons on). The rest of the night then became vague. I remember going to the toilet and I must have nodded off sitting on the pan. I can't recall being sick, just feeling knackered and falling to sleep. I was awoken by an American accent and looking up, there was this Yank peering over the top of the cubicle. *'You OK Buddy?'*. He got an attendant to open the door of the toilet, I thanked him and wandered into the club which was deserted. Chairs up on the tables with no sign of Nat and the two officers. I wandered out into the Calcutta night, there were just vague figures huddled in doorways. I stood there having not a clue of where I was and how I was going to find my way back to camp. Then a jeep pulled up with a Captain driving it. He enquired *'Where you going soldier?'. 'Dum-Dum Sir!'. 'Jump in before you get yourself assaulted or worse'*. He took me right back to the camp.

When Nat and I met next morning at breakfast, neither of us could remember much of the night before. He said they had looked for me and thought I had made my way back to camp. Nat wasn't sure, but he thought the two officers must have delivered him back in their jeep. So had I learnt my lesson of drinking Old John Barleycorn neat? You must be joking.

Chapter Fifteen

'Jackie Coogan and his Bar of Gold'

A story circulated by Allied servicemen around this time in Calcutta is too good not to re-tell. You have probably never heard of Jackie Coogan unless you're my age. So I'll introduce him to you. Born in 1914 in the USA of showbusiness parents he starred in a movie by the one and only Charlie Chaplin, the film being in the silent era. It was titled 'The Kid'. A story of pathos and humour - a typical Charlie Chaplin film. Jackie went on to star in many more films as a juvenile, being the top child actor of this time. So where does Mr Coogan show up next?.

He married the 'Oomph Girl' Betty Grable, an actress who appeared in countless films, but is best remembered as the No 1 Pin-Up girl of WW2. Every barrack room had a photograph of her in the men's lockers. The most famous being of her in a skimpy bathing costume in high heels and seamed stockings. Legs going upwards not knowing when to stop and looking provocatively over her right shoulder. Each leg insured for one million dollars.

Their marriage never lasted, they were divorced and Betty Grable went on to make very many films. One of the top stars marrying the big band leader and brilliant trumpeter Harry James. Jackie Coogan arrived in India with the 1st Air Commando Group in 1943 as an experienced pilot. He then flew British troops the Chindits under General Orde Wingate into a small jungle clearing 100 miles behind Japanese lines in the Burma campaign. No mean feat. It was at this time the story I am relating allegedly took place and knowing the Yanks I myself believe it.

He like many of the American servicemen liked his Bourbon and his rupees would run out. However, he had a bar of gold he carried around, in fact he was very much attached to it. It was the envy of all the Allied servicemen. They would never be able to own it, but for a fee they could look and admire it. It had been the delight of their No.1 Pin-Up girl Betty Grable.

So to set the scene the most popular Night Club in Calcutta at that time to all Allied servicemen was 'Firpo's'. So I would imagine that's where this story would have taken place. Jackie has run out of rupees and would retire to the 'Gents' remove his hat and find a dry spot on the floor placing the hat down. Word would circulate round the club that the show was about to begin and the men would crowd into the toilet throwing their rupees into Jackie's hat.

He would then, with a showman's flourish, probably turning his back to his audience similar to the pose of his ex-wife and swing round to gasps of awe from the envious servicemen. I never witnessed this exposure but I would think for a 'Few Dollars More' he would have let you touch it. The next time Jackie Coogan appeared was on the small screen in the 'Adams Family' with that ghoulish bunch of weirdos. He was Uncle Fester.

What a life. What a character. From the top child actor of the silent movies taking the title role in the film 'The Kid' opposite the legendary Charlie Chaplin. Marrying the top pin-up of WW2 Betty Grable. The legacy of that marriage leaving him with a Bar of Gold that kept him in drink. Then being a member (an applicable name) of the 'Adams Family' on the small screen. Also without doubt a War Hero as a pilot flying the Chindits into Burma. Jackie Coogan 1914-84.

Mentioning Burma I hope you'll bear with me if I recall another comical little story involving a one-eyed duck. You will remember the story of the chickens we had with us on our way down through that country. Well a couple of the Gunners had a one-eyed duck. The Urdu for one is Ek and for eye is Onk. So the duck's moniker was Ek-Onk. We stopped at this village with a pond and they had got Ek-Onk drunk on the hard stuff and because of his disability he used to walk side ways.

So here we have a drunken one-eyed duck walking sideways. I know how he felt through personal experience. He wandered into some oil or diesel from one of the lorries and got covered in it. So his owners gave him a good wash in soap then he decided to have a swim in the pond. Trouble was they had washed all the natural oils that ducks have in their feathers and he became submerged with his head poking up like a snorkel. I don't know the outcome, but I do know they rescued him.

Chapter Sixteen

'Ranchi and Two Weeks leave at Naini-Tal in the Himalayas'

The members of the old 56th Anti-Tank had been repatriated back to the UK so the Regiment were practically all new personnel. We had relocated to a town North of Calcutta named Ranchi, many roads converging on this fairly large populated town. The 56th set up camp on a hill a few miles out of the town with the main regiment on the front of the hill and the hangers-on. The REME (Royal Electrical and Mechanical Engineers) and us the Royal Signals, dismissed to the back of the hill away from all the bullshit. They had equipped the regiment with Half-tracks, meaning vehicles with wheels at the front and tank like tracks at the rear. The gunners main job being to keep them highly polished with every nut, and bolt painted a bright red.

It was bullshit at its worst and we were well out of the way, our two units were small. The REME had four personnel. We consisted of L/Cpl Charlie Elliot, Alf Palmer and myself. We also had a lodger in Nat Horwitz. I don't know how he had convinced the powers that be to let him bivouac with us, but he had. Some persuader.

Then a pleasant surprise for Alf and I. We were to have two weeks leave to Naini-Tal, a holiday resort for war weary veterans like Alf and drunkards to recuperate. They are termed 'Hill Stations'. It was to be a wonderful experience for us both. A once in a lifetime experience.

I had a very painful experience while stationed at Ranchi. I caught Dhobi Rash, Dhobi being Urdu for laundry. With all the washing being done together there it was a fair chance of rashes being passed on. So I got myself a rash from my laundry. Where?, but round my groin and private parts especially my scrotum. I scratched myself raw. So I reported sick and after the Medical Officer had a look at the offending parts, he sent me through to his Medical Orderly with the routine cure as this complaint was very common. *'Drop your shorts Mate'* which I did. *'Spread your legs'* I stood there at this masochist's mercy with my tackle exposed. *'Look up to the roof of the tent and grit your teeth'*. He painted my exposed parts with neat iodine, all round my groin and scrotum. I thought my testicles had been barbecued. Still it cured the rash and I couldn't go on parade as you can't march properly with your legs wide apart.

I had another painful experience at Kamaradi when I was stationed in the State of Hyderabad. We had several Piard dogs hanging around and when the units moved on, these camp followers were shot which was far kinder than leaving them to starve. There was a danger of catching Rabies from them as they were often carriers of this terrible disease.

I went to stroke a pup and it bit me so I had to undergo an Anti Rabies course which was very painful.

To our two weeks leave. We had a fairly long train journey then onto a three-ton lorry to take us 6,000 feet into the foothills of the mighty Himalayas. It was a a long winding road of hair pin bends and sheer drops into the valleys below, but far better than the roads we travelled over the Naga Hills. If you stared upwards at the mountainside they

The road winding up 6,000 feet to Naini-Tal 1945.

appeared to be falling in on you. There was a lady with a small dog that must have been doing just that as it was sick over her.

We arrived at Naini-Tal and were made comfortable at a hotel Tali-Tal House. We had our own Bearer to look after us, mine being Hari Ram. He called me the Ginger Sahib although I had no ginger hair. After the heat on the plains of India it was more like Shangrila than Naini Tal. The town is parked on the side of a very deep lake, so deep that the Navy with all its refined equipment was unable to gauge the bottom. The lake is a flooded extinct volcano.

The town in 1923 or 32 was swept into the lake with a landslide taking many of the townsfolk with it. Since then, there have been no motorised vehicles allowed through the town. There is only the one road on one side of the town, the other side of the lake going up a sheer rock face. Everything is carried by coolies on their heads. Their average life expectancy being twenty-six years. What an existence with just rags rapped round their feet - no Shangrila for them.

Our holiday was idyllic. Hiring rowing boats on the lake and strolling round it of an evening with lights dancing on the water and we befriended a couple of Merchant Seamen whose names I cannot remember, but with the sense of humour I appreciate. In one instance we were walking behind two Indian ladies and of all the races, you will never see anyone with better deportment than an Indian woman. I think the reason must be that they carry everything on their Uncle Ned (head). It was then that one of our nautical friends made a comment that amuses me now when I think of it. As I've said we were walking behind these two girls and one had very slender legs. He commented *'I bet she has a nice voice'. 'Why should you say that?'. 'Legs like a thrush'.*

Coolie Naini-Tal 1945.

Coolies Naini-Tal 1945.

Coolie Naini-Tal 1945.

Naini-Tal 1945.

Naini-Tal 1945.

One of the highlights of our stay must have been riding out early in the mornings on horseback. The horses were hired and they would be waiting for us after breakfast and we would ride up into the hills. Three of us soon got the hang of the rhythm of our mounts except Alf. The hardest was cantering where you raise yourself from the saddle in your stirrups. If you don't, the saddle hits you up the arse as you're coming down. If we had our bush hats on they would finish up over your eyes nothing like Clint Eastwood.

Galloping was the greatest fun, but not for our Alf. It terrified him galloping at thirty odd miles an hour with half a ton of live horse flesh at his command. That's if you were in control of it.

Number One Hundred

A little story of one escapade I had with one of the gee-gees. A lot of these horses were being rested from Calcutta race track. They had been out to graze for a period of time and then were sent to places like Naini-Tal to get them used to a saddle again.

At one end of the town there is a large square and the mounts were tethered at the far end, numbered from 1 to 100. Number 100 was a 16 hands stallion and to put it mildly he was a bit frisky.

On horseback 1945.

Many riders had gone off into the hills and 100 would come back riderless, dumping its rider a few miles up in the hills. I decided to have a go at breaking this bronco, fancying myself as a rodeo rider. I mean with my experience of a week surely I could master this challenging beast.

So I mounted up no problem and wheeled him round ala big John Wayne. Rider and mount as one. Then whoosh! we were away, the horse in full control galloping towards the far end of the square with a twenty foot wall coming up fast. *'Bloody Hell!'* I thought. *'Pull up you bastard'*. When we got nearly to the wall the nag dug all four heels in not for the first time probably.

Then calamity, the saddle slid slowly under the horses belly leaving me looking upwards and my head brushing the ground. Thankfully 100 didn't budge. I let myself slowly to the ground none the worse for wear. Since then I have managed a couple of horses and found that when you harness a horse it will blow its belly out, so you go back and take its girth strap up a couple of holes. Obviously this hadn't been done on this occasion with 100. Probably on a few other occasions which was why he was coming home riderless. After this episode 100 was withdrawn from the hired horses ranks.

Lucky for him I would have mastered him next time. Probably didn't want me to break the stallions spirit and make him useless for the race track.

'Dorothy's Seat' Naini-Tal 1945.

While we were in Naini-Tal we heard that a tiger had been shot in the school grounds - a story that would jog my memory a little later on.

It did sew a doubt in our minds about early morning rides into the hills, as we were riding what could have been Din-Dins for a large pussycat. We went up to the other side of the lake to a memorial stone 'Dorothy's Seat' erected by one of the townsfolk to his wife.

They had a dance at Government House and some of us were invited there to meet the Governor and the Dignataries' ladies and their daughters. Never had a

Government House Naini-Tal, India 1945.

chance to chat up the Burra Sahibs female offspring as they were closely watched by Daddy and Mummy. The word I suppose is chaperoned.

There were probably a couple that if they had played their cards right I would have danced with. So it was back to Ranchi and 120 F in the shade and army bull.

Himalayas 1945.

Every morning the regiment would fall in for Roll Call. Us the Signals had to send one representative, we sharing this privilege with the REME with just one between the two of us. It was my turn this morning and by the time I had got round to the other side of the hill they were all fell in. Just a couple of minutes late, but the guilty had to stand one side have our names taken and put on a CO's charge to be taken later on that morning. Now let me put you in the set-up. We the Signals were responsible for supplying lights to the regiment which included the Officers Mess, a large marquee. We had what was known as a Charhorse to charge 12 volt batteries up and deliver to the tents (we were under canvas) and connect same up. Now if the Artillery Officers got too stroppy with us, we would deliver a half charged battery to them and their lights would go out just at the wrong time. So they were in our hands. I'm sure you have the picture.

So we got our heads together for my alibi and I'm sure Nat must have been involved. He was now a full Corporal and studying Army Rules and Regulations to get his three stripes and be made up to a Sergeant Clerk. I helped him to review this very large book of A.R.A.R. as usual Nat mastered it and passed first time with flying colours.

So I fell in later that morning with the others on the CO's charge being taken this morning by the Adjutant, a Captain who had been wounded in North Africa. He always wore a yellow scarf around his neck, some said to hide the wound. He was an old sweat who wanted a quiet life. I was marched in, hat off to face him. The charge was read out. *'Have you anything to say in your defence Signalman'*. At the word 'Signalman' the Adjutant looked up. *'Yes I have Sir!'*. 'Silly question with my gift of the gab or Bunny Rabbit.

Now official time in the 'Kate' is not Greenwich Mean Time, but Royal Corps of Signals Time. So I pleaded that according to our Signal time the parade was called two minutes early. The wily old Adjutant got the picture straight away. He said he had checked his watch that morning and agreed with me that the parade had been called too early. *'Charge dismissed'*. I felt like winking at him but decided discretion was the better part of valour.

The others, the Gunners, go 7 days jankers and they weren't too happy. Tough! I learned to drive at Ranchi in a 15cwt lorry. No synchronised gear-box, you had to double-de-clutch. I drove from the camp to Ranchi with an officer who was testing me, which was straight forward and then it was driving through the town. The fastest vehicles being the Tonga wallahs on their bikes, but the main vehicles were carts drawn by bullocks so you hardly moved from the first gear. Anyway I got my pass. Handy when I was demobbed, as eight years later I got it transferred to a civilian licence.

One day a few of us went into Ranchi to the Forces Club. Amongst us was Nat Horwitz. We went upstairs to a dance floor with tables round it and sat down with a cup of tea. They were playing Big Band music over a tannoy system. There were a few couples on the floor. Mainly women dancing together probably officers' wives who were helping out at the club, and our Nat was eyeing them up for the best dancer.

She wasn't a young lady, but obviously knew her way round the dance floor. Now he excelled at the Tango which suited his Latin looks, he was quite tall and looked the part. I didn't see Nat approach whoever was playing the records, but he crossed the floor and asked the lady for the next dance. He led her across the floor with a flourish and the music started with the best well known tango of all 'Jealousy'. He flashed his 'Pearlies' at his partner and they gave a wonderful demonstration of this most sensuous of South American dances. The few couples who had been on the floor left it quickly to watch in admiration at Nathaniel and his breathless partner.

When the dance finished he led the exhausted woman back to her table and kissed her hand thanking her for the dance. There was spontaneous applause from the few of us that witnessed an Astaire/Rogers exhibition. Another memory to store in my mind.

I did see Nat a couple of times when we were demobbed, his family had a ladies lingerie shop in our local market. Those of you who know Walthamstow will be familiar with the High Street. Three quarters of a mile of shops and stalls, where the original Tesco's sold broken biscuits and as a kid, I would go to Manzie's pie and eel shop. This is where my brother Les and I would go Saturday mornings after going to the local cinema's 'Tuppenny Rush' to have our dinner and watch the man on the stall outside selling eels. They would be in these large square metal containers packed in ice and the customers would point to which eel they wanted. The poor bugger would be slit up, gutted and chopped up before you could say Saragosa (the area where the eels make their way from to the European rivers. Not a lot of people know that).

Nat opened a shop on the South coast somewhere and we lost touch. Thanks for the memory Nat Horwitz.

Chapter Seventeen

'Our Last Days in India'

Charlie Elliot and I found ourselves posted to a place I cannot find on an up to date map. It was near a village that was big enough to have a railway station. The place Kamaradi, was sixty miles from the second largest city in the state of Hyderabad. Name of the city Secundrabad. Again I cannot find this city on a modern map. I think that many countries after independence changed the names of cities, towns and villages.

We were a small detachment of the Royal Corps of Signals again attached to the Royal Artillery. Our main function was to operate a forty line telephone exchange linked up with the RA HQ just up the road.

Kamaradi, India 1945.
Left to right myself, Les Barnes, Doug Orson, A.N. Other.

There was a large lake near the camp - where the village woman would do their dhobi (washing). Bashing it against now very smooth rocks which the villages had been using for centuries for this purpose.

They often had a problem when big tribes of baboons would come down to the lake to drink and bathe. The women would huddle together as the baboons are liable to attack a single person.

Prior to Kamaradi I was in Poona for a few months. A lovely city as I remember it with shimmering white buildings and decent roads.

We were over-seeing the operation of wireless sets by Sikhs all in the Signals and very efficient at their job. Really they didn't need us as they were as good, if not better than us. We had the use of a small swimming pool mostly used by the officers' families and were billeted a couple of miles away in an old army barracks. We used to queue for our tiffin (grub) and have to walk across some open ground to the Mess Hall which was a large marquee.

Now throughout South East Asia and I suppose other countries, you will find these very common large birds of prey scavenging. They are I would think related to our Common Buzzard but we called them Shite Hawks.

A Shite Hawk.

We would wait for some new squaddies who had just arrived unaware of this threat from the skies. They would get their tiffin in two mess tins, they being square tins with fold-back handles a bit precarious and these innocents would walk across this open piece of land with their mess tins held out in front of them when WHOOSH! a Shite Hawk would hit the tins grabbing whatever they could with their talons. They have a three foot wing span and the new arrivals would have the rest of their nosh deposited over their new KD uniforms. It relieved the monotony, but they only got caught once and would cover their food over when making their way to the Mess Hall.

There was another incident worth relating. One of the men had a very large dog a Bull Mastiff which wouldn't let any Indian into our barrack room. He had to be chained up. Not a nice little pooch to have around.

One day one of the officers' wives' little lap dog wandered into our room unsuspecting this killer dog which grabbed the poor little mite by one leg and its jaws were locked. Everyone shouted to get the brute to let go to no avail. Up came this bloke who was obviously trained for this sort of emergency. *'Stand aside'* he ordered. The dog had a docked tail which meant it was just a stump. So this 'Obedience Trainer' in one movement got hold of the monster's tail and plunged his ring finger in this instance his middle one and shoved it up this unsuspecting dog's dirt box. It gave a yelp either in agony or ecstacy and released the small dog. You live and learn.

So I'm back in Kamaradi and another doggy tale. The first day I arrived with Charlie we were walking between our straw huts (bashers). Again heatwise we are talking about 120F in the shade and there was this mongrel dog tied up outside one of the bashers in the full heat of the sun. Most of the camp dogs in India were half domestic and half Jackal known as Piards, having pointed ears like the Jackals. I enquired whose dog it was and was advised to leave it alone as the owner was a nasty piece of work. So I gave the dog some water and released it.

Our canteen at this camp was a joke really, a larger straw hut with seats up each side and a small bar in one corner. I was getting to know my new comrades when this bouncy little bloke came in and silence fell. I weighed him up. He was only about 5 foot 4ins, but quite well built. In a broad Cockney accent he demanded *'Who let my 'effin dog off its 'effin lead?'*. I replied in my broadest Cockney *'I did mate'*. *'Right!'* he said *'The next time you let my dog off its 'effinlead I'll give it an 'effin good hiding'*. I replied *'OK Mush!, and if you give your dog an 'effin hiding I'll give you an effin hiding'*. There was silence all he said was *'Oh!'* He gave the dog away the next day to a more caring owner.

I got to know this cockney tough guy and we became quite friendly. I had read him right, the tough guy image was a con. He'd had a rough time as a kid being bullied so he turned his frustration on the dog. He seemed to turn over a new leaf and I became a bit of a hero to him afterwards.

Home Rule was getting near for the Indian population and it couldn't come quick enough for most of them. We had become like an Army of Occupation. After the way they had acquitted themselves in the war they had earned it.

Then another pleasant surprise, two of us were selected to go on a month's leave home. It was leave in lieu of re-pat. The two of us were another Londoner Les Barnes and myself.

We sailed from Bombay in the liner 'Canberra' back through the Suez again. I loved these leisurely boat trips. I'm sure much more enjoyable than a jet plane and the jet lag that goes with that. Up through the Red Sea via Aden, Port Suez, Port Said. The Canal looking much tidier now with no ghostly hulks of ships to be seen. Up on the deck watching the bow of the ship cutting through the blue of the Med and looking forward to my family and friends.

This was my third trip through the Bay of Biscay which had been very kind, but not this time. We had a rough passage. I stood on deck looking up a steep incline then minutes later looking downwards into an equally steep slope. Plenty of grub on the mess deck as hardly anyone was eating and what they did consume was soon airborne.

Suez Canal 1945.

So we docked at Southampton and I arrived home with my Ribbons and Bush Hat. Everyone wanting to hug me and kiss me. I made a point of seeing the blonde Lily, she was still going with this other lad whom she did marry as I stated earlier and I believe they had a large family. Also as I stated he became the youngest Mayor of Walthamstow. Dad was Joint Secretary of Walthamstow Avenue a Senior Amateur soccer side and my older brother Les played for them.

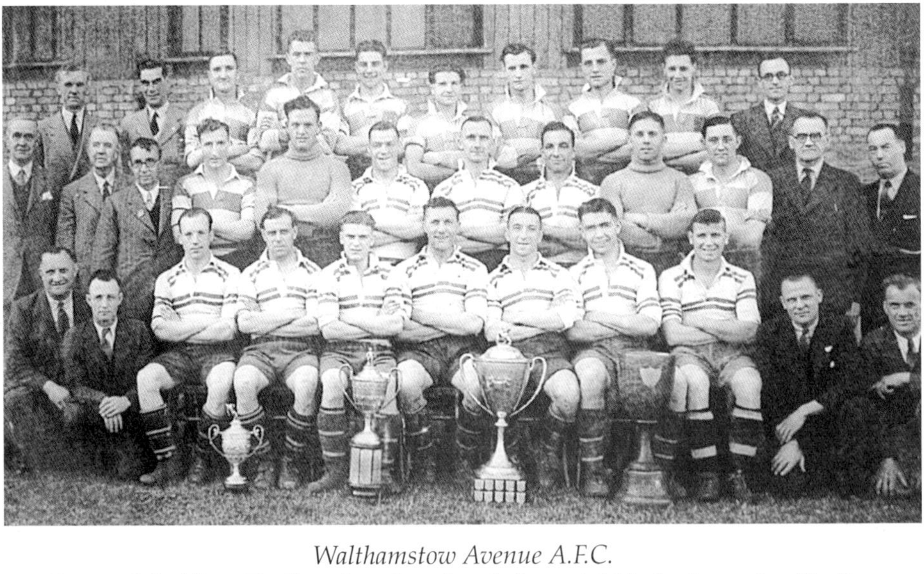

Walthamstow Avenue A.F.C.
Bottom left Albert Dudley, Asst Sec., fourth from right in back row Les Dudley. Father and brother of the author.

There was a dance being held one weekend at the club and a cousin of mine, who was in the Andrew (Navy) and on leave at the same time, accompanied me to this dance. He was over six feet with very dark wavy hair and of course in his Navy Uniform me in Bush Hat and new uniform. Rich pickings for any man-hungry female.

Dad introduced us to two young ladies whom I remembered from the Youth Club. One, Rene, a natural blonde (had enough of that colour) and the other with hair as black and velvety as night, Evelyn my future wife. We have now been married fifty-nine years in 2007. She always claimed the attraction was the hat and when I discarded it on demob, I lost my allure. Still married me though didn't she. Bit of a joker Evelyn. When I returned to India we corresponded regular. Best letters I ever had. So we embarked from Southampton on the same liner we came on, the 'Canberra'. On board were 500 ATS girls heading for the Middle East.

The two ATS girls and myself with Les Barnes on the right.

Les and I befriended a couple of them from Birmingham. The one that Les was with a little brunette. Mine a blonde (not again) who cried all the way to Egypt, the reason being that her boyfriend had been killed at Dunkirk and she had volunteered for this term in the Middle East in her grief. She then met up with another fellow having forgotten about her volunteering so things weren't going to plan. She was heartbroken and it was my shoulder that took the brunt of her heartbreak. To make it worse she had met up with a 'Nutter' me. There was an attraction for the ATS as we went through the Suez.

A road runs alongside the Canal with Arabs either walking or riding camels. When they saw the white girls on board up went their long clothes and they wore no pants, exposing their wares. The ship listed to Port with all the young ladies shouting words of encouragement like *'Get in there knob'* or *'Six out of ten for presentation'*.

So the 500 ATS disembarked at Port Suez, my blonde still weeping. I do hope things turned out the better for her and she had a happy life. Probably married one of those Arabs when she saw their tackle. So we arrived back 60 miles from the nearest town at Kameradi.

One day one of the straw bashers went up in flames and the Indian troops from across the way were over to our camp in a flash running through our huts picking up our belongings and dumping them away from the huts. We couldn't understand the panic as only one of the bashers was burning. *'All burn Sahib'* they were shouting and they were right, the sparks from the fire soon blew across, and the whole bloody lot went up in flames. We had the quick thinking of our Indian friends for saving most of our gear. We were equipped with large tents to accommodate four of us. They were square and we had managed to save our beds. These are called charpoys which are bamboo beds with ropes inter-twined to support you. Just a light mattress and a sheet with blankets when it dropped to 80F in the night.

Doug Orson with an ape.

In our tent was Doug Orson from Malden, Les Barnes, a young lad from the sticks and myself. A rope tied round the tent to secure Mosquito nets to and a Bearer for each tent to keep the place tidy, clean our boots and lay the bed out for a Rupee from each of us. A king's ransom to them. I know that the Indians were glad to get their own rule and decide their own destination. They had had enough of the British Raj after all those years, but the British Army gave a lot of employment wherever they were in India, employing thousands of people directly or indirectly. A lot of them probably finishing up begging to join all the others in that soul destroying way of life.

Discipline was very lax as everybody was looking to return home and one day a 3 tonner was laid on to take us to a private house with a swimming pool. There were three WVS at HQ, Womens Voluntary Service. They did a marvellous job throughout the war in every area of combat. Two of the ladies were sisters the other an older person about 40 years old which to me at 19 years appeared senile.

So the three WVS were on this little 'jolly' with us to the swimming pool. On inspecting the swimming facilities we found snakes in the pool, but were told they were non-poisonous. They were laying under where the perimeter of the pool's paths overlapped the water, they were there to keep the insects down. Did we go for a dip? You must me joking.

The older woman for no apparent reason apart for my obvious boyish charm and bronze physique, took a shine to me. When we got chatting she was an interesting lady having travelled much. She had spent several years in South America and when I introduced myself as 'Ronald', I became 'Ronaldo' her tongue rolling over the 'R'.

It was lovely talking to her and we found we had a lot of common interests, other ranks never got the chance to meet a British woman or indeed talk to one. I mentioned the fact that I had a fortnight's leave in Naini-Tal and she burst out *'Oh! that's where Jim Corbett lives'*. I was bemused as my Jim Corbett was 'Gentleman' Jim Corbett - at one time heavyweight champion of the world. I couldn't believe this gentle looking lady was in to fisticuffs. She explained that her Jim Corbett was a hunter of man-eating tigers, then I remembered we were told while at Naini-Tal of a tiger shot in the school grounds. He was often called on by the Indian Government to track down and kill these big cats that terrorised whole communities for several years. The villages in remote areas of the Himalayas with a man-eater often killing over one hundred natives, not only tigers, but leopards.

This very generous lady loaned me a beautiful bound book entitled *'The Man-eating Tiger' of Kumaon'*. It stirred an interest in the subject mainly about Jim Corbett that I still have today. His books of which there are several, I now have in paper back which I never tire of reading. His knowledge of the jungle and the fauna that live there are described with so much interesting detail as well as his confrontation with the killers. Laying in the fork of a tree over a recent kill of the man-eater for hours on end. Cramp in your legs and listening for the slightest rustle in the undergrowth. Coming eyeball to eyeball with one of these killers.

So I have to thank this lady of so many years ago for introducing me to the world of Jim Corbett and I cannot even recall her name.

During our time at Kamaradi I had two weeks leave to come so I decided to spend it at HQ. This was before I had met the aforementioned lady so forget it.

Had I conquered my drinking habit of neat whisky? I leave you to judge. There was a fence around the perimeter of HQ and a Sergeants Mess was just on the other side of this fence. I found a breach in the fence and spent the whole fortnight in the Mess in a mess.

There was a film made some years ago with Ray Milland and I believe he won an Oscar for his part in it. The film was entitled *'Lost Weekend'*. He lost it in a drunken stupor the whole two days. I knocked that into a cocked hat as I lost two whole weeks of my life to Old John Barleycorn. I would find my way back through the fence, find where I was sleeping and collapse onto my bed. Someone would wake me up to go for some grub. Goodness knows what meal I was eating if I kept it down, but I would go back to my hole in the fence and carry on drinking where I'd left off.

So back to Kamaradi to our Signals Unit and some of the characters in our camp. Most of them with the sun were a bit Dulali which is another place that seems to have vanished off the map. It was very hot there and the sun would grill your brains as in most places in India. Fortunately it never affected me.

Meet Jock our Storeman. Obviously a Scotsman who had lost count of his marbles and as puggled as they come. He had a pet green parrot which never left him, always perched on his Uncle Ned (head). Jock had a thick mop of curly hair and he didn't look unlike Harpo the dumb Marx brother who played the harp. (For those interested in real life, he wasn't dumb).

There were about twenty of us on the payroll and a brand new Second Lieutenant. A nice enough bloke fresh out of Sandhurst or wherever they come out from - lovely white knees. Also a young Sergeant, who like the Lieutenant, didn't want any trouble. It was the usual performance of roll call and inspection. They would inspect those of us who had got up and bothered to parade. The parade was outside the stores of which Jock was in charge which consisted of his charpoy and a few odds and ends.

So he would be fell in and there would be old barmy Jock with his parrot on top of his head. He would saunter up as if he was doing someone a favour unshaven and his hair matted with parrot's shit which he would massage in and to be fair, he had a lovely shock of hair a good advert for parrot's shit and a filthy uniform.

He would glare at the sergeant and officer daring them to say something about his appearance. Names would be called out and when it was Jock's he would say *'Good morning Sir!'*. *'Thank you Jock'*. The young officer would be glad to get it over with for another morning.

The young officer came from London and I popped in with a letter from him to his parents, also to assure them we were looking after their lad when I had that leave.

Back to Jock. Now and again they would have a Whist Drive at HQ and a 3 ton lorry would be laid on for those interested. If you've never played at a Whist Drive, you play with a partner. This would be myself and Jock plus the parrot. The cards are dealt and the trump suits are played in rotation starting with Hearts. Normally you play to win as many hands as you can with the winners moving up and the losers moving down.

At the end of the night the partners who had won the most tricks were declared the winners. Those with the least won the booby prize.

Jock and I being of like twisted minds, used to play to have the least tricks at the end of the evening. Believe me this is far harder than trying to win. You pick up your hand and have a lot of trump cards. Your partner puts a middle trump card on the table and you put a higher one on top of his, bearing in mind you have already won the hand. This is where acting ability comes in, apologising to your partner for over trumping his card.

After a while the other players would realise what we were doing and maybe think the parrot was giving me some sort of signal. Did we ever win the booby prize? No never.

Another barmy bastard was a little fat geezer who worked in the Motor Transport section. The lights which came off a generator would go out at say 2300 hours and as they dimmed, this little prat would wind up his gramophone and give us a blast of 'The Entrance of the Gladiators'. There was no volume control on his turntable gramophone, but there would be shouts of *'Shut that bloody noise off'*. This circus would be repeated every night, bit of a laugh really. I was on the forty line exchange one night. The basher where it was situated was one of the few away from the others that hadn't burnt down. There was the front office where the officer and sergeant worked, then a dividing wall to the exchange that side. A charpoy for you to kip down and a low battery powered light on all night.

You would make your bed up for the night making sure your mosquito net was well tucked in, otherwise the mossies would have a feast off you. Sometimes your arm would lay against the side of the net and you'd be covered in their bites in the morning. Another hazard were these large flying beetles. They must have weighed an ounce and would hit the side of your net at night. If they hit you they would have stunned you. It was when they landed on top of your mosquito net - you had problems. They would urinate on you and this would form a large blister on your leg from the acid. If this burst, wherever the liquid ran, another blister would form.

I don't know the Latin name for these flying Bulldozers, but we called them 'Piss Beetles'. Not very imaginative, but apt.

It was my turn to man the exchange one night, I had made my charpoy up and as it was quiet, I thought I'd go for a cup of char to the canteen, which was a large marquee that was falling down. As I came back into the front office I could hear the weights on the ends of the cables that were used to plug into the exchange to connect callers jangling. When I went through to the exchange half of the basher, there was this Royal Artillery Major trying to connect himself through on the exchange and his large German Shepherd dog was under the exchange causing the jangling. As I came through the front office I had grabbed a pencil. *'Where have you been soldier?'* he barked at me (the man not the dog) *'Sorry Sir! I broke the lead on my pencil, and went to the front office for another'. 'Your not to supposed to leave the exchange. You're on a charge'*. This incident was previous to when I had the month in Blighty and it could jeopardise my leave if he charged me and I was found guilty of leaving my post.

I explained the situation to our officer and he got in touch with his immediate superior a Captain Jones an Anglo Indian. I had told our officer that the Major was interfering with the exchange so he had overstepped his authority.

Captain Jones contacted the Major and told him that if he insisted in pressing the charge against me, he would have to bring a counter charge against the Major for interfering with Signals property in breach of Army Rules and Regulations.

Myself and 'Nicky'.
Doctor: 'How long have you had it?'. Monkey: 'It started as a wart on my arse'.

I was told to report to the Major and he was very polite saying that as I was due to go on leave we would forget the whole matter. (Whooped again). We had a couple of pets in our tent in the shape of a Chameleon, a most fascinating and a very small monkey who was very jealous of the aforementioned reptile. He actually hated the sight of it and would go spare if we paid too much attention to it. We had tied a rope from the two tent poles that held the tent up and the Chameleon would balance along it moving very slowly then it would flick several inches of tongue with a sticky blob on the end catching insects. The monkey's name was 'Nicky'. I can't remember if the lizard had one, probably 'Lightning'.

We decided to go to the pictures one evening. These were open air affairs on somewhere like a football pitch at HQ. You took your own seat and could sit either side of the screen, so some of you would view it arse about face. We had put Nicky under a tea chest and he had a harness round his waist with a light rope attached to it. So we tied the 'rope' to one of the tent pole and propped the tea chest an inch or so off the ground for air. Then off we went.

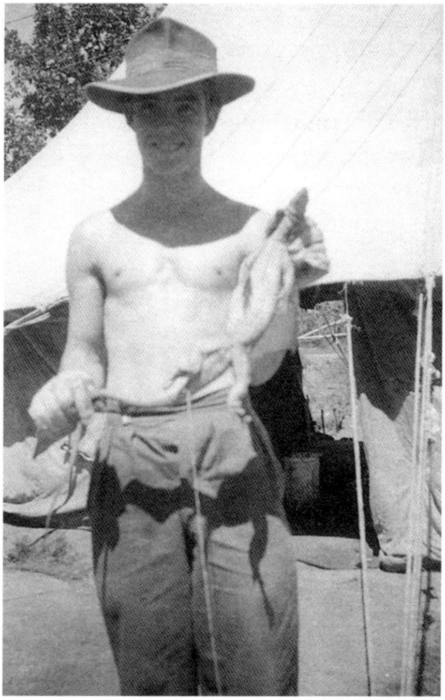

Les with iguana lizard, Kamaradi 1945.

When we arrived back at our tent, there was the monkey chattering away and all we could find of the Chameleon was its body which had been de-capitated but no Uncle Ned (head) anywhere. I leave it to your imagination what had happened. It seemed Nicky had got his little hands under the gap we had left under the tea chest for him to breathe, lifted it up, shinned up the tent pole and bit the lizards Uncle Ned off. We never found it so he must have eaten it. Les wanted to give the monkey a whack but the other three of us would have none of it. Nature is very cruel and at times hard to understand.

We had another encounter with a reptile when the Indian troops from across the way came charging through our camp in hot pursuit of something that was crashing through the undergrowth. They were wielding sticks. Whatever it was took cover in our tent under Les's charpoy. It was an Iguana about two feet long. Not big as iguanas go, but big enough.

The Indians grill them over an open fire turning them on a stick. They say they taste like chicken. My thought was then why chase the poor bloody lizard, why not buy a cooked chicken. Les was very protective of it and when the Indians realised that they weren't going to get the Iguana, they dispersed and Les gave it its liberation in the jungle behind our tent. When you arrive you hear about all the insects, reptiles and other poisonous creepies, but you soon learn to cope with a routine of knocking your boots out in case a Bootlace Snake had decided to get its head down in your daisies (daisy roots - boots) for the night. The Bootlace Snake is the Asp of Cleopatra fame, a very small black reptile and Bootlace aptly describes it, but very venomous. In the old bashers which we occupied before they burnt down there were Rat Snakes, a Viper that lived in the roofs of the huts. About five or six feet long but comparitively harmless to humans as they were constrictors. In the flaps around the walls of our tents small Scorpions would make their home.We had a large mound behind our tent which was home to a Whip Snake. We were told they were nocturnal but if disturbed, they would spit their venom at your eyes a bit like foreign soccer players.

Chapter Eighteen

'Back to Blighty'

A photo of myself and my dear old Mum. Taken in 1945 with me kitted out to return to India.

So the day came to pack our kit and make our way to Karachi where we spent a few days before boarding the liner 'Georgic' for another 6,000 mile sea journey home. Les Barnes was also on the draft. Another pleasant cruise across the Indian Ocean to Aden through the Red Sea to Port Suez, into the Suez Canal. Then to my mind, the most pleasant parts of the trip sailing through the Mediterranean. Past Gibraltar and through the Bay of Biscay which again behaved itself. Docking at Southampton for the last time, I estimate that I have clocked up about 26,000 sea miles and another 10,000 land miles in my travels to India and back, four times on the ocean. Then from Bombay to Mhow to Jorhat over the Naga Hills down through Burma. From Rangoon across the Bay of Bengal to Calcutta. Indirectly to the Himalayas back to Ranchi onto the State of Hyderabad stopping off at Poona before finally arriving back to Blighty's shores and seeing the White Cliffs of Dover and the green fields of home.

Did I enjoy my travels? Read these memoirs and judge for yourselves. My army service hadn't finished yet as we had a short leave and Evelyn and I got better acquainted but nothing really serious yet. She visited Mum and

Dad every week. So I found myself in the spa town of Harrogate or just a few miles out of the town in a quiet camp with most of the personnel like myself waiting to be demobbed. When I attended the first parade, I was asked if I would like to work in the Sergeants Mess and I declined the offer.

The RSM, a real old sweat took me to one side and spoke to me very friendly. *'Now come on son. You'll be out of the army soon and in the Mess you'll eat the same as us. No parades and plenty of time off Cushty! you know it makes sense'*. Touch of Del Boy.

So here I was, a waiter in the Sergeants Mess and it was as the RSM promised a cushy number to finish my service. There were two of us and the cook who we only saw at meal times. The other waiter and I had our own room in the Sergeants quarters just the two of us. We didn't see each other much. Ships that pass in the night.

He was a friendly enough bloke whose sister was courting a Yank and he used to show me these silk ties the American gave him with hand painted palm trees and Hawaiian hula girls on them. He also told me that at weekends to leave biscuits and two cups of tea outside the RSM's room.

I used to get a bus into Harrogate, a clean town with a café and cinemas. I went to a dance one night and there were two girls dancing together. One very attractive who turned out to be the local beauty queen.

Myself and Ev.

A full Corporal and myself had a verbal bet who would take her home. No contest. I cut in on the two girls before he knew what was happening and we glided into a quick-step. I can't remember if he tried to cut in, but forget it son and watch a master at work, taught by the one and only Nat Horwitz. Her name was Fay and I would take her home that night. Again no fooling about as she was courting and I had my thoughts on Evelyn. Fay was a very lovely pleasant girl who made my short stay in Harrogate a pleasure.

Back to my waiter's job. I did as I had been told, to leave biscuits and two cups of tea at weekends outside the RSMs room which I did and I could hear girlish giggles from the other side of the door. I'm sure that wasn't the RSM. He was also due for civvy street and they say he would be in tears not looking to the prospect of civilian clothes and looking for a job. The British Army had been his family for maybe thirty years and they were kicking him out on the street. He was always civil to everyone in the Sergeants Mess and was well respected. I hope the poor old bugger got settled maybe as a Chelsea Pensioner. Two cups of tea and biscuits outside his door week-ends as he was having a game of crib with a mate.

I was sent to the City of York to collect my demob suit and snazzy trilby hat. The suit was a dark serge pin stripe and I looked like a Pox Doctor's clerk. I am coming to the end of my young conscript's tales of his exploits in far flung countries which I hope have interested and amused you. I will finish with a tribute to one of my comrades in arms.

Chapter Nineteen

'Tony Mercer L/Cpl Royal Corps of Signals'

When I had settled down to the now-boring routine of civilian life, Evelyn and I pledged our troth. In other words we got married. Ev had a very good job in the City as a Clerical Officer in War office BMA Buildings, Tavistock Square, London. I went back into another factory with other men who were getting demobbed by the thousand now. I was employed as a fitter, but not for long, another story.

I had told Ev about Tony Mercer and I was sure he would surface in the entertainment world. He had been travelling with a revue 'Hello from SEAC' in the far East from 1945 to 1947 and sang with some of the British Big Bands when he was demobbed.

We now had a television set in our two rooms over my parents and there was a circus from the Blackpool Ballroom with Reginald Dixon on one of those cinema organs. A trapeze artiste swinging from a trapeze - what else? and a lovely ballad 'Laura', then it happened. This deep rich Baritone voice, Ev I blurted, that's the Tony Mercer I have been on about.

Then in 1952 George Mitchell formed the *'Black and White Minstrel Show'*. Tony was one of the founder members of this show, appearing at the Victoria Palace in London where it had earned the distinction of being the most often performed musical show ever staged in London.

We were now living in Essex having moved out from London when my brother Les visited us. My Dad was the joint Secretary of a well known senior amateur football club, Walthamstow Avenue, where Evelyn and I had met. Les also played for the club as I've stated before.

The club had organised a trip to see the *'Black and White Minstrel Show'* at Victoria Palace would we like to go? So we found ourselves in the front row

The author's father Albert.

waiting for the show to start. I gave girl who was selling cigarettes and ice cream a short note to give to Tony. It just said: *'Ron Dudley 56th Squad Catterick out front'*. My Dad the ever pessimist, *'He won't remember you'*. The girl came back to tell me that Tony would see Ev and I during the interval backstage. He had put on some weight since our service days, but he said *'He remembered me well'*. We had a lovely chat about Catterick and South East Asia Command. He asked us to meet him after the show which we had to say no to, as we were with a coach of other people. He took Ev's programme and got signatures to treasure which she has to this day.

I never saw Tony Mercer in the flesh again. Then the tragic news that he had died, the circumstances were very sad. His only son was the organiser of a large scooter club and he was responsible for collecting thousands of pounds for charity. He was involved in a road accident and was killed. It broke Tony up as he idolised the boy and he was very proud of him. One thing led to another and as I've said he died tragically.

He was a nice fellow who gave a lot of pleasure to a lot of people one of them being me. I have my Black and White LPs and another that he recorded with a large orchestra arranged and conducted by Brian Fahey. Rest in peace L/Cpl Tony Mercer.

Tony Mercer.

Chapter Twenty

'The Road Back to Civvy Street'

Sequel to 'The Road to Rangoon and Back'

Before I got demobbed, my girlfriend Evelyn and I got engaged. She could obviously see what a good catch I would be when I returned to civilian life. I had done my best to impress her by being slightly drunk on our first few dates and having no money, so she had to pay for the cinema tickets. She also kept me in fags.

I managed to get a job after having a month's demob leave and found myself working in a factory again. We would go out weekends with three other couples on tandems. One being my brother Les and his wife Peggy.

I remember the first time we went out. Evelyn had never done any form of cycling before, where I had cycled miles. The eight of us on the four tandems covered about a hundred miles and the missus was shattered when we were several miles from home. This left me to push the tandem home on my own with Evelyn with her feet up behind.

We were living in two small rooms over my parents and Ev staggered up the stairs and collapsed on the bed face down. After I put the bike away I mounted the stairs and there was my young wife of a couple of months lying on her front with two very large lumps inside her thighs. Blimey! I thought she's had a sex change. It was of course caused by her legs chaffing on the saddle of the bike.

Myself and Ev on one of our cycling trips.

After she recovered we spent many glorious weekends cycling over many miles. Fishing rods tied to the crossbar and going angling at Sawbridgeworth and Roydon in Hertfordshire. We would go to the London Palladium to see the shows also the athletics at White City Stadium. However I felt trapped after the army. My one regret ever since was the fact that when I was at Kamaradi, I was offered three Sergeants stripes if I signed on for five years. I had always felt comfortable in the army and I would have had a decent pension.

The Tandem Club - on the right myself with wife Evelyn (behind) and sister-in-law Peggy.

Evelyn had a very good position, working in the War Office as a Clerical Officer. There was me a lowly fitter in a factory. When I was a kid our family would have a holiday in a small village several miles from Colchester with my Uncle Arthur and Aunt Harriet.

I loved it and they would leave me at Layer Breton Heath for another four weeks. Laying in the long grass listening to the grasshoppers. Watching the Skylarks dropping like a stone from high and trying to find their nests. My biggest thrill was cutting a stick and going rabbiting when they were cutting the corn with those old harvest binders. As the binder got towards the last few cuts, the rabbits would panic and start running in all directions. I would manage to catch one sometimes and march home with it hanging from my stick like a Red Indian brave returning from a hunting expedition. Could I do it now? No way José. I've mellowed in my old age and will even move a snail from the drive in case I run over it.

Evelyn and I had a few holidays at Layer Breton. We both loved the tranquillity of the countryside and the slow pace of the life. So I started taking the farmer and stock breeder answering ads for farm workers to no avail. I finally put an ad in. *'Young energetic man seeking to get a farming position. Muscles of an ox with a brain to match. Anything considered'*. I had six replies and after sifting through them answered one in Suffolk.

I can't say whether Evelyn was all that keen with her job and its excellent prospects, going to live in the wilds of rural England. We met Miss Mills the Manageress of the farm and it was snowing. She picked us up at Bury St. Edmunds railway station. We arrived at Giffords Hall which was six miles from the main road.

On the way up the drive to the big house we passed these three cottages. The farm had been there for 400 years. With all the buildings listed, some listed more than others as you shall see. It was owned by two sisters with a niece living with them and as I've said managed by a woman.

'Giffords', Suffolk.

We were taken to the dining room and the butler brought our dinner in. There was a bit of meat on the plate but the pièce de résistance was a very large swede dominating the whole proceedings.

A memory that sticks in my mind was whilst looking out of the window onto a lawn with a large tree and watching some small birds pecking about, a Sparrow Hawk swooped down and took one of the birds. We finished our dinner with the blood sport entertainment and were taken down to the three cottages that we had passed on our way to the main house. The three were still occupied. The middle one would be ours. The other two, one occupied by the butler whom we had met and the other by the foreman whose cottage we were taken to. We met Fred Atkinson and his wife. He also had three boys. They were very nice people and showed us around their abode.

As I've commented, the cottages were 400 years old but with lino down and being furnished they didn't look too bad. Very large beams in every room which Ev and I didn't give a thought to at our peril. So we accepted the job and the tied cottage. Wages £4-10 shillings old money. Six bob a week rent. The big perk of the first pint of milk from farm cows free, but any further we would have to pay for. I would be looking after two horses.

So we moved off to Wickhambrook in Suffolk with our brand new furniture and into our 400 year-old home for a year. Under the foreman's lino the floors were just rough cobbles and the wooden beams were full of woodworm. Our lighting was an Alladin oil lamp. There was fresh water from a tap from the farm's private supply. With no mains electricity, cooking was by oil stove. The removal men put our bed up for us and were gone as it was still late winter and they had got lost coming with snow still on the ground.

400 year old cottage at 'Giffords', Suffolk.

Evelyn and I were both tired after the journey in the cab of the lorry and decided to go to bed. We sat on the side of the bed and Evelyn started crying. *'What's the matter Ev?'*. Her response was *'What the bloody hell have you got me into'*. Now remember how I told you that all the buildings were listed. Well our cottage listed from the centre to the outside that our bed started sliding in that direction towards the outside wall. We both finished up laughing. In fact we couldn't stop and we have some very enjoyable memories of Giffords. If you have the AA book Treasures of Britain, turn to page 207 and there you will find Giffords Hall Suffolk.

Back to the bed wandering about the bedroom. I had to put some books under the front legs to keep the bed level and we had to lie very still. You must be joking.

Fred the foreman had a lifetime with horses and my only experience was number 100 at Naini-Tal. He taught me how to harness the 14 hand high pony up, to put in a two-wheeled cart to take two churns of milk up to the main road and bring two empties back. The other horse was an 18 hands Suffolk Punch being 21 years old. He pulled a heavy two wheeled cart. Both horses were geldings.

'Punch'.

It was very hard manual work and I got as fit as I've ever been spreading muck by hand with a four tine fork and loading the trailer up with bales of hay using a two tine fork.

One amusing incident with the bull that the owners had purchased. The milking herd were Jersey's and they paid a lot of money for this young Pedigree bull. He was covering the cows and heifers but they weren't getting into calf. So they sent for the vet to check his fertility (no not the vet's). How? you might ask as I did. Well, when a cow comes into season (I hope I'm not getting too technical) you will see one cow mounting another. The one cow is in season, or what a herdsman would call 'bulling'. So we waited for a cow to start bulling and sent for the vet.

When he was ready to take a sample of the bull's sperm, we let him mount the cow (the bull that is). The vet then produced a long glass tube with a bulb on the end and placed it over the bull's penis catching the sperm. He then took a smear onto a small glass plate and placed it under his microscope. After studying it carefully he invited Fred and I to have a gander. Explaining there should be thousands of small black organisms wriggling about whereas there were hardly any.

Now someone had the unenviable task of explaining this to Miss Mills and also to the two old maids up the house. *'Well Miss its like this. You know how tadpoles hatch out into frogs. Well the bull has no tadpoles'. 'Oh! you mean that the bull is firing blanks'.*

Anyway they had to take the farm who had supplied the bull to court to get their money back. I wonder if they had to go through the procedure with the bull and cow performing in court? (and of course the vet).

One night there was a film showing in Wickhambrook village hall and I took Fred down on the back of the tandem. It was about eight miles away and Fred lapped it up.

Taking the pony George down to the main road with the two churns on the float and the farm dog Gyp following us this morning, I heard them in the distance. The hounds and the huntsmen coming towards us. Now George used to go with the hunt but because he was pigeon-toed he was retired as a riding horse.

Author with his father in the float with George in the shafts.

His ears pricked up when he heard the huntsman's horn and all of a sudden we were surrounded by these bloody great dogs with Gyp in the middle joining in the fun. The bloke with the horn could see that George wanted his head. *'Let him go man'* he shouted.

So I threw his reins over his back and we were away with me trying to hang on to two empty churns. As we neared the farm I remembered that there were about two hundred cockerels in a large wired enclosure just by the side of the road. The dogs smashed the chicken run down and there were these cockerels that were being fattened up for market being chased by the hunt dogs. They must have run all the flesh off their bodies and finished up like Road Runners.

I was spreading muck in a field after breakfast and I could hear the hunt a few miles away and spotted them all on the side of a hill. I couldn't believe then what I saw. The fox was some way in front of the hunt and this is perfectly true another fox crossed the line of the other fox laying a fresh scent. The hunt followed this decoy fresh fox which was full of running.

Not so long after I saw the original fox run along the hedge at the top of the field where I was spreading the muck. I wonder if he found one of those afore mentioned cockerels?

I went up to see Fred one day when he was cleaning the bull pen out. He would take his belt off and put it through the bull's nose ring and tie this to one of the pipes around the enclosure. There was Fred merrily getting on with his chore and I spotted the bull was loose. I told him and he dived out of the bull pen with the bull chewing away merrily at the hay that Fred had put in his trough, wondering what all the fuss was about. The bull had also chewed through Fred's belt to liberate its self.

There was one animal on the farm that was very fertile in the shape of a ferocious Rhode Island Red Cock. It was running with about one hundred hens and it was nasty. Anything that trespassed on its territory it would attack including the portly butler. It would lay in waiting for him in the mornings as he was going up to the house and grab his legs.

The niece of the owners had named it Alexander the Great and she doted on it. It attacked Fred's youngest son ripping his legs up. That was his swan song or whatever is the last song cockerels sing. Fred caught it and tied it up by its legs to a beam in the stables. As he was finishing it off the niece came in and accused us of torturing Alexander. Watching Fred dispose of the cockerel it was done very humanely by an expert. He must have killed many chickens in his time working on farms in Britain and Canada where he spent many years.

The highlight of the week for Evelyn and I was bath time. Let me take you around our cottage. There were two bedrooms as I remember or was it three? Downstairs was our kitchen. Cooking on an oil stove and a sink. Our toilet was in a big room with just the pan in one corner with a cistern, as we did have a water supply, but to warm our bath water up, it was heated in a large copper outside in the wash house. Our bathroom was a very large spare room that we hadn't got enough furniture to use it as a sitting room.

Taking you back to the toilet. You would be squatted in the corner in this room that was big enough to hold a whist drive in watching large house spiders scurrying about the floor. I always felt like Little Jack Horner sat in the corner, but I wasn't eating my curds. Just disposing of them and hoping the spiders weren't the funnel weaver. So back to the bathroom. Our bath tub was one of those long metal bungalow baths. In one corner of the room was an old cupboard which we didn't use so I drew a dartboard on one door and would amuse myself throwing darts at it.

So we would heat the water up, lug it into this large room and fill the bath up. Evelyn would have the use of the water first and I would be in the queue waiting my turn. As we used just the one lot of water and me being the gentleman, I would wait my turn.

To help me pass the time I would throw a few darts at my dartboard and Ev would panic as I'm not very accurate with the arrows, and she would admonish me with *'Watch where your throwing those darts'*. Laying there naked I suppose she had a point. Or was frightened of getting one.

In the end cottage the butler and his wife lived and they were members of the Salvation Army. She would get Fred's three boys to move one of those old fashioned organs that you pumped with your feet onto the forecourt then she would hand out hymn sheets and the boys would sing. After the session was finished she would give the boys those small text cards with a psalm on them.

During the week the youngest boy, a little angel, would pinch the flowers from the butler's front garden and plant weeds in their place. The flowers would be re-planted in their own garden. I didn't mention our small living room that we spent our evenings in. Our entertainment was a battery driven radio and we would listen to the 'Archers', an everyday story of country folk. Made a change I suppose. We didn't keep late hours as we had to conserve the oil in our lamp.

I have to tell a little story and I hope you'll forgive me if it offends, but I often think of it and it still amuses me. Also employed at the farm was Jim the gardener a nice bloke and his assistant old Walter. He was a grizzled old countryman probably in his eighties who didn't say too much.

Remember the eighteen hands, twenty-one-year-old Suffolk Punch work horse, well Walter was there when our old Punch was born. So to get round to my little story. I can't remember the occasion, but Fred was in the tractor pulling the trailer which Jim, Walter and myself were sitting in. Walter broke wind very quietly and commented *'That was a pretty little thing'*. Every time I remember that scene it brings a smile to my lips.

After one year at Giffords the farm went broke and I had to find fresh employment. It was the high wage they were paying me that sent them into liquidation.

Miss Mills gave me an excellent reference and I applied for a cowman's job in Essex near the village of Finchingfield. Very well known with its pond in the middle of the village and often seen on chocolate boxes and calendars.

The farm was several miles from Finchingfield, the local town being Braintree. The owner of this fairly large farm was a gent named Bowen Roberts. He was a Gentleman Farmer in every respect. Educated at either Cambridge or Oxford and he was a double Blue. He took Evelyn and I to view our future home. The farm was known as Petches.

Our tied cottage was two storeys and thatched with mains water for drinking and washing in. The toilet was a small shed outside like you see in the old Westerns. A long bench like seat to perch on with a bucket underneath. The trapdoor where you pulled the bucket from to empty it was missing with just a sack over the opening. Not exactly draught proof.

The cottage was semi detached and the other house was occupied by an old farmhand Herbert and his wife. The half that would be for Evelyn and I was still occupied by the departing cowman, who took me to one side to warn me *'That bloody Pole will kill you'*.

Apparently Bill the man I was talking to was the under cowman as I would be and the head cowman was Joe, a Polish immigrant. This was in the early 1950s. Bill had about six offspring. Evelyn and I had a meal with Mr Roberts and his wife. We were left alone to discuss the job and the living quarters. Oh! yes my wages would be £11.50 a week and no rent.

We had no intention of returning to London so we decided to take the gamble and move to Essex. I hadn't met the infamous Joe as of yet, then I met him on my first morning at work.

As I've said he was Polish and his full name was Joe Sadownik. I found out that you pronounce the 'W' as a 'V' so Joe's surname was pronounced Sadovnik. He was around six feet tall and all muscle and bone, not a bit of waste on his frame. Now I had worked with some very strong men, but none stronger than my new workmate.

The first morning my job after milking (which I'll come back to later), was to take all the utensils used for milking wash them and sterilise everything.

There were four large pots that held four gallons when full. Everything was worked by suction. Taking one pot to explain as good as I can how the system worked. There was an air pipe that ran the whole length of the milking parlour driven by a large compressor in a shed outside. There were one way taps staggered along the length of the parlour where you plugged the milking machine in.

So back to the actual milking machine made by Alfa Laval. The pot had a lid on with one long tube connected to four cylinders which were rubber lined. These slid over the cows four teats, one in each corner of her udder and the milking done by a pulsator connected to the four cylinders. That's as simple as I can explain it.

So after milking I had to strip the four machines down, wash everything thoroughly in a large metal sink. All the rubber tubes had to be cleaned with a long slim brush. In fact everything scrubbed, then all put in a big metal steam steriliser and left for a few hours. There was also a cooling system where the milk ran over a corrugated metal appliance. This also had to be washed and sterilised.

Going back to the actual milking of the cow. You placed the four cylinders over the teats and when the machine had stripped as much as it could from the cow, you massaged her udder to take all the milk out. If you left any milk in, the cow could get Mastitis or worse still, Milk Fever. The milk feels like a jelly in the udder and it takes a little while to get the feel of it.

After milking, Joe and I would take all the cows down into one of the many meadows laid to grass and then go off to breakfast. I had a two-mile walk back to our cottage and would have a very large fry up for breakfast. We started work at 5.45am and were usually home by 8.00am.

We would be back down to the dairy buildings by 9.00am. While I washed and sterilised the milking machines, Joe would clean the milking parlour out. A very manual job. Loading all the cow dung onto a four-wheeled trolley and pulling it across the yard to unload it. Joe would hose the four-wheeled trolley down and we would load the churns of milk onto it. There were usually ten churns, each holding ten gallons of milk. A churn of milk weighs 100lbs and with the weight of the churn this would be well over a cwt.

We would take the loaded trolley out to the road and put the churns up onto a platform about four feet off the ground. So you had to lift a churn up by one handle and swing it onto the platform. This was my first test as far as Joe was concerned. Could I lift 140lbs with one hand and lift it two feet onto the platform? After the heavy manual work I had been doing at Giffords for 12 months, I was in good condition. I had always been strong physically since humping weights in the factory. I realised that Joe would be judging me on whether I could keep up with him work-wise.

I had little trouble with the churns, so I had passed my first test. I can't say Joe was alienated towards me. Here was a man who had left his family to settle down in a foreign country. His English was very good and he had married a local girl from Finchingfield. I suppose the word I am looking for to describe his attitude toward me was suspicious, he may have thought that I was after his job. That first morning after we had unloaded the churns, was to fill a large wooden container in the milking parlour with cow cakes. These were compressed goodies in a cube about the size of an oxo cube. I followed him to a large Dutch barn where the feed was kept and they were in bags of 56lbs. Here was my next test.

Joe picked up one under each arm to walk about 30 yards to the parlour. Bill's words came back to me *'That bloody Pole will kill you'*. So I got two of the bags one under each arm and followed Joe to the parlour. Second test passed.

I still hadn't had a proper conversation with him.

Milk fever in a cow's udder could mean that she could lose that quarter, if the cows were dry. In other words they had given their quota of milk and were now in calf again they would be put out to grass for a few weeks until they were due to calf again.

Then was one old lady Annette who we brought in to calf and one quarter was rock hard. So the vet was called and he had to clear the channel in her teat up to the udder.

He had this instrument that had four blades which closed into the pencil like body when you inserted it into the canal of the teat, but when you pulled it out the four blades opened up to cut four slits up the canal of the offending teat. Makes your eyes water.

One thing about cows that is different from other quadruped or animals with one leg in each corner like mules or horses. They just kick backwards, but a cow can kick both ways forwards or backwards. I was taught that when I was milking a cow, to put my shoulder hard into the cows back leg then if she kicked it would be just a push. If you were away from the leg and she lashed out towards you, the milk container, and you, would finish up in the cow's feeding trough. If the cow had either milk fever or more commonly mastitis, where the fore milk that you strip out before you put the machine on is lumpy, you had to inject penicillin into the quarter into the teat contained in a tube similar to one of those super glue tubes. Going back to old Annette she lost that quarter.

Mastitis wasn't all that common if you were careful when you stripped the cow out. We had one cow that would kick backwards as you passed her and we had to put bales of straw behind her in case.

Mr Roberts had moved some two hundred chickens down onto the meadow in front of the farmhouse and whoever was milking that evening had to shut the hens up. Why you may ask?

I came on one morning at 6.00am and there were chicken corpses all over the meadow. A vixen fox and her cubs had slaughtered nearly all the chickens. Just biting their heads off.

So who was the guilty party? It was the boss who had a house party the night before and hadn't heard all the squawking that must have gone on when the foxes were ripping the chickens' heads off.

Evelyn and I would often go down to Finchingfield village hall to watch a film. It was just a make shift screen and ordinary seats arranged in lines.

There was one comedian who would come to the film show, I believe his name was Gary. He was a big bloke of over six feet and his mate was a little fellow of about 5 feet 2 inches. They would come to the pictures on a two-stroke motor bike. The little chap being the driver and Gary riding pillion. It was comical to see this giant of a man sitting behind this midget of a man on this equally small bike. Now friend Gary was a verbal comedian.

We went to see this sad film one evening and all the ladies had their handkerchiefs out dabbing their eyes. It came to a very sad scene. You could hear a penny drop, but it wasn't a penny that dropped, someone broke wind loudly and Gary shouted in a loud cockney voice. *'I'll have a fourpenny one'*. After that there were loud guffaws and prim ladies tittering. The whole atmosphere changed from sadness to laughter.

One day Joe called me into one of the cow boxes. He was in there with Mr Roberts. Joe said that Mr Roberts told him we weren't spending enough time on the farm. We were spending about sixty five hours a week sometimes more with cows calving and so on. I don't think that Mr Roberts wanted me in on this conversation with my rabbit.

So I said that he was quite right and Joe looked at me. I went on that we ought to bring our beds down and sleep here.

Mr Roberts grinned and the outcome was Joe and I got a farthing a gallon on the milk we produced. It doesn't sound much, but at one hundred gallons that's 25p a day £1.25 a week. Remember we were only paid £11.50 a week. Joe was chuffed.

Then after about four days when I was washing the milking equipment, Mr Roberts came into the dairy to ask me how I was getting on. He told me that Joe had complained that I was taking too long in washing the utensils and sterilising them. This was right up my street. I replied *'That there were two ways of doing this very important job, which if it wasn't done properly could cause all sorts of problems. Leaving stale milk in the rubber tubes. Causing a bacterial problem'*. I continued *'I could do it properly or quickly. How did he want me to do it?'*. Remember I had only been here for a few days. Mr Roberts grinned *'Point taken Ron. Do it properly.'* Joe never said anything to me but the boss must have told him my reply.

So we carried on and I still hadn't broken Joe's iciness down. Then my chance came. I went into the dairy one day and there was Joe studying the form of the horses. I looked over his shoulder and enquired if he liked a bet? He was just writing a betting slip out. *'Can I have a couple of bob with you Joe'*? I felt a relaxation in his attitude. I had a look at his slip and suggested having a bet of up and down double stakes about. This really impressed him.

When I was working in the factory before I got called up in 1944, if you remember I was courting the tea girl. Well her father was the stoker at the factory keeping the boiler going that heated the whole factory. I often had a bet with Charlie on the Gee-Gees. He had served in the Merchant Service and was a hard old sea dog and it was he who told me how to lay this complicated bet out. The local bookie was the butcher in Finchingfield and when we took the bet to him he wouldn't accept it, not knowing how to work it out if the bet came off. So I suggested we have an each-way bet on a long shot and if it came up, double the stakes onto another each-way selection. I can't remember whether we won anything, but I had won Joe over.

Next thing, Evelyn and I were invited to meet Joe's wife Barbara and her brother and his wife. We spent many evenings in their company playing cards. Joe and I became very good friends.

About the herd of cows that we were responsible for. There were sixty milking cows and usually forty followers.These being young heifers and young bulls that had been castrated to become bullocks that would finish up at the knackers yard. Now British Freisans are one of the heaviest milk yielding breeds. A mature cow can give up to ten gallons a day, that's a whole churn full or 100lbs.

I remember one old lady that was yielding over ten gallons a day, the heavier milkers having to be milked three times a day. Mr. Roberts would also milk. So two weeks you would be milking two nights, this included week-ends. On the third week you would be milking three nights and that would be your weekend off. So two weeks you would be working 60 hours and on the third week just a little less, all for £11.50 a week.

Believe me when you went to bed at night you slept as you were up at 5.30am the next morning. If a cow was due to calf, she would be shut in a calving box behind the milking parlour. This night I was on and we had a first time heifer very near to calving.

After I had finished milking and had turned the cows out into the meadow, I went to look at the heifer and she was having problems. The calf coming out back feet first. This could mean losing the calf as the umbilical cord would break and the calf would suffocate.

The vet was phoned for and he had been forewarned. He was there promptly. He was a very big man, but said we would need some help. This was at the weekend I went up the hill from the farm about 5 minutes run.

So I went to Geoff the tractor driver's house and they were all out. I knew that next door an Irish family was living there and banged on the door. This well dressed Paddy came to the door enquiring what the problem was at this time of night.

I explained we had a calf stuck could he help us and he joined me on the road. I suggested that he should change but he wouldn't hear of it. He looked as if he had been out drinking.

As we were getting near the farm buildings I asked him if he had pulled a calf out before and he assured me he had. I took him through the milking parlour round the back to the box. Mr Self the vet had secured a rope to the calf's back legs that were protruding from the cow's rear end.

I looked at our Irish friend and he was goggle eyed. *'Sure I thought we were going to pull a car out from some mud'*. With my London accent and his Irish brogue we had got our lines crossed. The vet explained to him that when he said 'Pull' we were to pull on the rope downwards which is very important. If you pulled directly outwards you can damage the heifers internal organs.

Anyway the calf slithered out and I quickly cleaned its nostrils out of mucus to make sure it could breathe. A brisk rub down with some dry straw and the heifer turned to lick her first offspring clean. Poor old Paddy couldn't believe what he had been a party to. I'm sure it was a story he told over a couple of pints many times.

Mr Roberts asked me one day if my wife would be interested in becoming a domestic working in the farmhouse.

Remember Evelyn had been working in the War Office as a Clerical Officer and he was asking me if she would like to become a skivvy. I was going to say scrubber which is not detrimental. They were the ladies who scrubbed the steps of the big office buildings in London. So I arrived home that evening and told Ev I had secured a position for her. *'Doing what?'*. She questioned me. When I told her she spluttered. *'You must be joking'*.

After some thought she said the extra money would come in handy. So my Evelyn swallowed her pride and went to work for Mrs Roberts in the house. They also employed an au pair girl.

Our cottage was getting a bit dodgy with the thatch full of sparrows and I asked the boss if it could be re-thatched and it was. It was also covered with wire mesh over the thatch to stop sparrows and rats making a home of it.

Ev and I then applied for a council house. Mr Roberts was very helpful vouching for us and being a farmer, this meant a lot with the council.

It wasn't too long before we were offered a brand new bungalow in the village of Great Bardfield, a fairly large village about the same distance from Petches as Finchingfield. In sport there was a lot of rivalry between the two. I had been playing cricket with Finchingfield along with Mr Roberts who had a Blue in this game.

Another farm employee was the farm bailiff Mr Sharp. He was a slow right arm over the wicket spinner and the opposition would attempt to cart his little dollies out of the ground at their peril, missing the ball and getting stumped.

Before we leave the tied cottage on the farm a few memories. I was given a chicken house and we had half dozen hens which not only kept us in eggs, but the Egg Packing Station would pick the extras up, which meant they didn't cost us anything as with the revenue from the eggs I used to purchase the corn to feed them.

The one thing I didn't like was emptying the bucket from the toilet. I used to beg Evelyn if we had visitors not to give them too much to eat or drink.

On one occasion it was Evelyn's sister Sylvia and her husband Alf. Sylvia swore blind that because of just having an old sack over the trap door at the back of the toilet she got piles. So this discouraged her from using the bog. Was I going to make a proper wooden trap door? No way.

After they had said their goodbyes I thought I would empty the bucket that held about four gallons. When I slid it back out to empty it, it was brim full slopping about all over the place. I had already dug a hole in our large plot of garden ready to receive the offering. Try carrying a brimfull bucket of excreta and urine without it going down your legs. I tried to hold it away from my body and when I reached the hole, I had to hold it up high so that it didn't go all over me. It descended into its resting place and one small drop hit my lip. I had rubber gloves on and couldn't wipe it off. I went to the back door of our house and Evelyn was in the kitchen. I was pouting my bottom lip a bit like that chef who shall be nameless. *'What's the problem?'* she enquired. I mumbled *'Agh! Agh!'* pointing to the offending drop of urine on my bottom lip and she hasn't kissed me from that day onwards.

As I mentioned earlier, electricity had just been wired into our two semi-detached and our next door neighbour Herbert was terrified of it. So much so I had to change his light bulbs as he thought he would get an electric shock by just removing the dud bulb.

We had a Sales Representative come into the milking parlour one afternoon after we had finished milking, but the cows were still in their yokes waiting to be turned out.

To tell this yarn properly, let's go back to the Suffolk farm Giffords. My brother Les and his wife Peggy were visiting and we went out for a walk. Coming to the field where the cows had been turned out to, some of the herd were walking backwards. I ran back to inform Fred the foreman of the weird goings on. It was spring time and the cows were out on fresh green grass. If they eat too much of this the gases in their stomachs will swell and will kill them. They control the amount the cows can get at by erecting an electric fence allowing them to eat just a little every day and then moving it forward into the fresh grass after they had cleared that part of the field.

What had happened? Taking the cows down the lane to the field they were in, they had loitered eating the fresh spring grass each side of the road. So after stuffing themselves before they had reached the field, they had over eaten and were now suffering for it.

We drove the herd back to the yard in front of the cow shed and waited for the vet to show which he did in a short time. So the cows' problem was the expanding gases in their stomachs of which they have three and the gases had to be released or they would die. The vet produced what I would describe as the pea-shooters we played with as kids. These had a bayonet type pointed rod that went down the middle of the pea-shooter and the mouth part of the pea-shooter had two holes each side and two long lengths of cord past through them.

The vet felt round the cows stomachs to find the offending stomach, then plunged this instrument in right up to the hilt. He then removed the bayonet from the centre leaving the pea-shooter in the cow and tying it round the cows stomach. Immediately the gases started bubbling from the tube, green gunge and gases. He repeated this on all the blown cows and saved all of them.

So we travel forward in time to the Essex farm Petches and the Sales Representative all done up like a dog's dinner. Smart suit, smart tie and shirt, polished shoes, in fact everything a good Sales Rep would wear.

Now the cows had been out on fresh grass and you passed too close behind them at your peril.

Let me introduce you to old Nanette, probably the oldest cow in the herd. A dignified old lady with half her tail missing and a weak stomach. I was conducting our Sales Rep through the milking parlour and he was just passing Nanette's rear end, when her stump of a tail went up and she coughed. Old matey got covered in loose cow shit, in fact the old lady filled one of his pockets up. We did the best to clean him up doing everything but hose him down. I don't know what sort of reception he had from Mr Roberts at the house.

So Evelyn and I moved to our brand new bungalow in Great Bardfield. Before I move on, while we were at the tied cottage my Dad Albert came to stay with us and brought Sam down, a cross bred Spaniel pup. He became one of us. He loved coming out over the fields with me and hunting rabbits, something we would both miss when we moved into the village.

Evelyn finished her domestic job at the farmhouse with no regrets. There was a family grocery shop in the village owned by a gent named (now don't laugh it was his name 'Clinkscale'). The job was much more to Evelyn's taste and was a stepping stone to much better things. I used to go out setting snares to catch rabbits and was getting quite good at it; watching whichway the grass was laying in their runs till one day I came across someone's snare that had been forgotten.

The rabbit was in it and had died an agonising death with the large birds probably Magpies pecking its eyes out while it was still alive. That was it for me, I went round taking all my snares up.

Another time I was taking Sam out for a walk and we were sat on top of a small rise watching a family of rabbits at play. They were chasing one another running round in circles without a care in the world. Then a pair of stoats appeared, the female much bigger than the male. The male joined in this game of ring a roses with the naive rabbits and the doe stoat just sat still watching her mate performing this dance of death. He managed to single out one rabbit and mesmerised it. He gradually worked it away from the others with his mate ready to pounce and kill, albeit a lot quicker than a snare.

It was then that Sam lost patience and went running down to this show that nature was putting on. The stoats scarpered as did the rabbits except the one that was now away from the others and still under the spell of the stoat. As Sam got near, it pricked up its ears and was gone.

It took me back a few years when I was fishing with rod and line. Nothing moving. The float not bobbing indicating a bite when there was a skirmish on the opposite bank and a water vole came sliding down what looked like a well-used slide. On its tail was a stoat. When it saw the water it went into reverse with its four legs rotating backwards. It was like something out of a Walt Disney cartoon. The hunter did manage to stop before it hit the water.

I had purchased a bike to get to work and Joe and I were still having a wager on the gee-gees. I was still going home with Joe to enjoy Barbara's country cooking. The job was bloody hard work but I loved it, feeling a lot fitter than I feel now.

I'm sure some of the aches and pains I now suffer were caused by the heavy lifting I did when I was younger, but another in a desk job would blame his back problems on sitting down all day. We were now getting to know the Bardfield village people. If you passed one without an acknowledgement you were a stranger.

Evelyn was settling in nicely into her shop assistant's job. Mr and Mrs Clinkscale were very kind to her. I was approached to play for the village football team, the reserves that is, on my weekends off.

Evelyn and I joined the Badminton Club in the village hall, a game I enjoy. There were dances in the hall, strictly ballroom at which Evelyn and I are quite proficient. In fact we were getting absorbed into the village culture. Then a hiccup, I contracted a rash. It was a wet rash and under the doctor's advice I had to wear long gloves in bed as the rash would weep during the night and I had to peel the gloves off in the morning. They irritated terribly but I actually stuck it for a whole year and was sent to a specialist in Braintree. After having various ointments tried out with no success I was told that I was allergic to the cows after three years. I was so upset. Working with animals was something I had always wanted to do and now I would have to leave them. I did experience some gut wrenching experiences. One was when it was decided that some of the older cows that were not giving much milk and not earning their food, would have to go.

One morning we were told to leave about six of these old ladies in their yokes after the others were turned out. Old Nanette was one of them. She only had one and a half horns and of course her stump for a tail.

Joe and I put some extra food in their troughs for them and they were chewing away contentedly when the knacker men turned up with the Humane Killer. One minute there they were waiting to be milked then the spike was driven through their heads and their feet just collapsed. I know that big hard Joe was just as upset as I was.

I was off one weekend and they had the vet out as they had X-rayed one of the cows and discovered she had swallowed a small length of wire. How? It's just one of the dangers of tying bale up with wire. So picture the scene. The cow was tied up in her yoke and the vet administered a local anaesthetic. Joe was looking over his shoulder. The vet got a scalpel made three incisions where the wire was shown on the X-ray cutting a three sided square. He dropped the flap of the cow's skin down exposing her innards. It was then that Joe slithered to the floor spark out, he had fainted.

A happy ending though as the vet located the piece of wire and removed it and the cow recovered with no after effects. Joe? When I heard about it I never mentioned it to him.

Back to the six old ladies. I did notice that Mr Roberts kept a low profile that day. When they had culled the cows the knackers men backed their lorry up to the parlour and unwound a steel hawser from the back. They tied the back legs up and just dragged them up to the back of the lorry. It seemed a so undignified way and a poor reward for the service they had given to man. It wrenches my gut now when I picture it. Maybe the rash was a blessing and I wasn't cut out to work with cows, but no, I wasn't to give up yet.

Mr Roberts was very understanding with my situation and it was fortunate that we were not still living in a tied cottage. I had no intention of giving up my cowman's job yet and heard there was a milking job going on another farm. I thought maybe it was the herd of cows at Petches I was allergic to. So I applied and got the job with a retired army officer Captain Cook.

It was a fruit farm and I would be solely responsible for a small Jersey herd. I did explain to the Captain about my rash problem and he said he would chance it if I would.

So I bought myself a two stroke James motor bike to get to work on. Captain Cook had two sons working on the farm, both easy enough to get on with. As I've said, the farm was a fruit farm employing men and women to pick the apples and prune the trees. It was one of the lady pickers who acted as my relief on the milking when I had a weekend off.

It was of course a seven day a week job as working with animals is. She was a married woman with a couple of children. Mabel was exactly what you would expect of someone working out in all weathers with lovely red rosy cheeks.

We had a very young bull there, a Jersey as all the herd was. He was too young to cover the cows yet but he was aware of what nature was all about and if women passed near his enclosure, he would bellow out loud.

Mabel went in to feed him one day and he pinned her against the side of his pen jumping up and placing his front legs over her shoulders. She swore he tried to rape her, which I had no doubts about and she refused to go in with him again. I've met a few women who would have jumped at the chance.

I went in early one morning and there in front of the milk parlour doors was a rabbit with its head swollen up and eyes popping out of their sockets. My first experience of Myxomatosis. That terrible virus that was introduced into this country to wipe out the rabbit population.

I remember during the war the rabbit was one of our main food resources. One stall in the Walthamstow High Street was all they sold, hundreds hanging up on the stall to fill our bellies. You will not taste anything better than baked rabbit cooked in onions.

Having said that they could practically ruin a crop of wheat, eating large corners from a field, as will a flock of wood pigeons. When the disease was rife to bring a South American Bob Tail rabbit into the UK was a punishable offence, as they had built up an immunity against the virus as have our British strain now over the years. Changing their life style in the process, abandoning living in burrows and making their homes in the hedgerows. Having said that I don't know if they have now gone to ground again.

I was now having problems with the rash again and the Captain employed another cowman in case I had to finish, which I did in the course of time.

My new partner was a very well educated man. He had been working in a young offenders institute, teaching them to rehabilitate, learning about cows and herdsmanship.

He was about my age and he wasn't all that friendly towards me with my Cockney accent. A barrier I intended to break down, but how? I remember it was a Saturday and it was John's turn to work the weekend. I said Cheerio! to him and he looked very miserable with himself. He liked a cigarette and I knew he was out.

When I returned 30 minutes later with ten fags he just couldn't believe it. His face lit up and the barrier he'd built up was demolished. After that John couldn't do enough for me.

He was living in Finchingfield with another ex college graduate and also his own girl friend. Evelyn and I went to a dance in the village hall with George and Connie our neighbours in Bardfield and John and his friends were there. I thought now is the test, would he introduce me to his lah-di-dah friends or ignore me. When he spotted me, he brought them all over to our table. *'This is my good friend Ron who I work with'*. It was a very good night in what turned out to be excellent company.

So I had to find another job away from the cows. I had become friendly with Pete who lived a door but one away from us. He was a self employed bricklayer along with another man. He offered me the job of labourer, mixing the concrete, hod carrying etc. Bloody hard work. They had jobs all over Essex and Hertfordshire. Pete had a motorbike and side car, I would ride in the side car and we would pick Alan up in another village. The three of us got on very well together, unlike the start I had with first Joe and then John. Is it something about cowmen? Only I was one of them.

I was with Pete and Alan for three months before the work dried up mainly as it was now Winter. They were both embarrassed when they had to lay me off, but Pete's brother-in-law Albert was the foreman on a very large farm which was mainly arable. He took me on as a tractor driver. Over the Winter months I was also hedging and ditching which is self explanatory. Cutting the hedges back and burning the cuttings as you went. Then clearing the ditches out of all the rubbish that had clogged them up during the year.

I quite enjoyed the job apart from chopping the sugar beet out. This was an agonising job, the hardest I have ever done. The beet would have been sown in rows about two feet apart. When the seedlings had grown big enough you went through them with a hoe leaving just three or four in small clumps about four inches apart. After a couple of weeks you went through them again to leave a single plant.

I had done just a little at Giffords, but I couldn't keep up with others who were born with a hoe to play with in their prams. I managed to do nine acres. Three of them I went through twice as the farmer told the foreman I hadn't singled them out properly. You got paid by the acre so I didn't get paid for the extra work.

All the farm hands were living in tied cottages and had also worked for the farmer's father and they all pulled their forelocks and called him Sir!.

Evelyn and I then decided to buy a brand new car, a Ford Anglia. I sold the motor bike and turned up at work one Monday morning in our new car. I was given my notice at the end of the week as I hadn't chopped enough sugar beet being the reason.

A couple of days later I saw Albert's car outside Pete's and walked along there. Before this I had spoken to a neighbour Jack, asking him how many acres of sugar beet did he expect to do in one year. Remember I had done 9 acres, 3 of them twice. Jack told me in a good year he would do 6 acres. I told him how many I had done and had been put off because I hadn't done enough. Jack couldn't believe it.

So I confronted Albert as he had been given the job of giving me my notice, with the reason that I hadn't chopped enough sugar beet. He apologised and said that his boss didn't like an employee turning up for work in a new car, as it would make his other hands restless.

Albert was allowed a car as he was a cripple and he had to get about the farm. You have to admire a man like Albert.

So where to now? I couldn't go back to milking cows because of the rash which incidently had now cleared. I decided to look in the papers and saw a job in Dunmow, a town about 10 miles away. It was for a fitter in a development factory, owned by the biscuit manufacturers Scribben and Kemp. There was no way Evelyn and I would now move back to London, having carved a new life out for ourselves. She was doing very well for herself as I shall explain soon.

We talked it over and the one big factor was, I would be earning much better money and I now had my own transport to drive the ten miles to Dunmow. I went for an interview with a Mr Halsey the development engineer and got the job.

There were about twenty other men and women working there, with several of the men being Londoners.

So let's get back to Evelyn working at the grocers. Mr Clinkscale was a lay preacher and out of the blue he and his whole family, wife and a few children emigrated to America, I believe to follow his religious calling.

Evelyn carried on working as a grocery assistant and a temporary Manager was sent from Braintree. Then a position in accountancy turned up in the Braintree office which Evelyn applied for which because of her training she succeeded in getting. There were three girls travelling to the town every day and they offered Evelyn the spare seat paying her share of the petrol cost. Things were going very well for a skivvy. Then another opportunity arose for her.

The Co-op were looking for a permanent Manager for the grocery shop in the village and they actually offered her the job because of her experience in the shop and knowing the customers. They were also impressed with her proficiency in dealing with accounts. So she was now the Manageress at the village shop. How was Ron getting on in Dunmow?

Mr Howes the development engineer had designed a clever electronic machine for testing the weight of packets of biscuits. It would reject them if they were overweight or under weight.

It was sent to a Machine Exhibition at London's Earls Court and I went with it as I had built it from scratch. Let's give the factory a whiff. Let me introduce you to the Morris family who lived on the corner just down the bottom of our road Benlows. A lovely family who Evelyn and I got very friendly with over the years. There was Dad Frank and Mrs Morris, four boys. Jimmy, Ernie, Peter and Billie. Then two girls, Rosemary and Gillian.

The four boys were very good soccer players and Pete became a special mate to me.

I remember when I first met him I was in Little Bardfield a smaller village just a couple of miles away and talking to some of the lads from the village. They were full of the fact that one of their village heroes, Pete Morris was now home from the army. I was on my two-stroke motor bike, he approached us and I was introduced to him. A good looking lad with a jutting determined chin and like all the Morris family, blond apart from Mum who had flaming red hair. Nice firm hand shake which I always look for and the most pleasant grin.

He asked *'How about a ride on your bike mate?'*.

I dismounted my steed *'Why not mate?'* and off he went just a little way up the road. I think he was surprised that a total stranger would trust someone he'd just met with his new bike.

As you can see I was still working as a tractor driver before I got the push and purchased our new automobile. I used to visit the Morris's on a regular basis and was always made welcome. At the time none of the offspring were married.

Frank the father was an ex Rugby League player which is probably why all his boys excelled at sport, all playing for the village cricket and soccer teams.

I was fascinated how the household chores were handed out and all the offspring had to muck in. I believe there was a rota. One day you would be washing up, then hoovering, bed making and so on. I have never been in a happier house, the atmosphere was so inviting.

Three of the sons were employed by the local builder bricklaying, but Billie the second youngest of the boys had a white collar job in Braintree.

This one day I went down to visit and have a cup of Rosie Lee (tea). There was some banter going on between Frank and Billie who had purchased a watch which was waterproof, shockproof and every other proof you could think of. He had got it at a bargain price.

As it was guaranteed to be waterproof, Frank had bet his son that it wasn't. He was offering Bill a wager that if they got a bucket full of water and submerged the watch, it would leak. Bill's reply was only if his Dad submerged his wrist watch as well. I watched the older man's face which said it all, he had a wide grin right across it.

So the watches were suspended on two lengths of string and down they went simultaneously into the bucket and everyone crowded around. Nothing at first then Billie's watch sent a stream of small bubbles up to the surface.

Everyone was laughing including young William. I don't know if he had his money back from the person who sold it to him, but I do know that he had to pay the bet.

Frank worked on the big American Air base at Wethersfield another village just up the road from Finchingfield. I had many happy hours on the base in the NCOs canteen. That's where I was first introduced to drinking whisky topped up with 7 UP, a Canadian type lemonade. By diluting the hard stuff you could drink much more. There were also those massive T bone steaks, meat on the hoof. Evelyn came home one day from the shop and said that a couple had moved into living quarters over the shop. The husband, an American Airman from the base and his wife, British from Newmarket in Suffolk.

They would hold parties regularly inviting a lot of the villagers including Evelyn and I with plenty of grub and plenty of booze. One afternoon we were all at Emmy's and her husband's at one of their parties and Ev who doesn't drink a lot, had too much and was bad and I mean BAD! Feeling sick. I had to take her home which was only five minutes away.

I sat her on the side of the bed and placed a bowl between her feet. I legged it back to the party as I couldn't do anymore for her could I? She has never let me forget this incident. Never could hold her drink.

Going back to Bill Morris. He bought himself a new pair of football boots in town and during a game they were crippling him. When he came off at half-time he found the shop had sold him two boots for the same foot. It always happened to Billie and you know what, it was always met with a wide Morris grin.

We went to my cousin Jean's wedding when she married a Yank from the base and as they had nowhere to go for their honeymoon we invited them to stop for the weekend at our place in Bardfield. They were still there six weeks later.

Her American husband was about 6 feet two inches and was on the slim side for a Yank but he loved his booze and he would bring home cartons of beer. Andy and I would sit there into the early hours yarning and drinking.

I came home one day, Evelyn and my cousin Jean were in a state as Andy had come home Brahms and Liszt (pissed) and was in the toilet. It was locked on the inside. There was just one of those small windows and I managed to look in and he was lying on the floor asleep with his Uncle Ned (head) on the toilet pan. I managed to slide the lock across with my fishing rod rest. The door would you know, opened inwards. After a long struggle I managed to extricate Andy from the toilet and wrestled him onto the bed. They finally got a home and moved out.

While I'm on about our American cousins, I will introduce you to Ewell Williams who married the daughter of the lady who lived opposite us in Benlows Road.

They had a couple of children and I had never met Ewell. What a character. He came knocking on our door one evening holding a fish up on a line. *'Hi!'* he announced himself. *'Could you tell me what sort of fish this is as it bit me'*. It was a small Pike. I told him its Grandaddy would have taken his finger off.

From that introduction we spent many hours fishing on Gosfield Lake a few miles away. He drove a German Ford. I believe it was called a Taunus. He was a brilliant driver, having driven since he was a schoolboy. He told me that his family lived 100 miles from their nearest town and it was a long straight road. They would do the trip in one hour flat, just foot down all the way.

If we weren't getting a bite, Ewell would practice an old trick they would use from where he came from in the deep South of the States around the Mississippi. He would go to the back of the boat and urinate the water and sure enough our floats would start bobbing. I can visualise it now with an International Angling Match being shown on the box and as there were no bites everyone is reading 'The Road to Rangoon and Back' and they all reach this chapter, unzip their flies and tinkle, tinkle.

He was telling me once that he would go down to the Mississippi to catch these giant Catfish they eat in that part of the world. This was when he was just a kid. He would accompany a large Negro lady who would catch plenty of the fish with no problem. Ewell asked the lady what he would have to do to catch the fish. *'Well Honey when you do catch a fish you must remember how your mouth was, and hold it like that all the time'*.

So in time Ewell did manage to hook a Catfish but couldn't remember how he had his mouth at the time.

So there would be this young boy sitting there with his line in the water distorting his mouth to all sorts of shapes to find how it was when he hooked his first fish. One day we all went for a ride with Ewell. That was his wife, his mother-in-law Rosie, Evelyn, their children and myself. We took the old Roman Road from Bardfield to Dunmow.

If you are not familiar with this road and the chances are you are not, it has many twists, and turns. There is one part that practically turns back on itself called Dead Man's Corner. Several years ago a motorcyclist was killed there.

So after taking only an hour to travel one hundred miles back home, our American friend was getting a bit peeved with this old Roman Road a 'twisting and a 'turning. His ma-in-law was explaining that she had heard a documentary explaining that when the Romans built these roads, they always worked with their backs to the wind. So we reached Dead Man's Corner. This was too much for Ewell.

He exploded *'Must have been an effin whirlwind when they built this stretch'.*

So many amusing stories to tell if only I could remember them all. I was asked to go onto the Village Hall Committee, meeting in the Doctor's house. This is where I met George a very intelligent man who approached me one day. He had come into possession of a very large Silver Cup that had been presented for prize Dahlias. His idea was to have all the engraving removed and have a football competition amongst the surrounding villages, calling it 'The Great Bardfield Cup.'

So we called a meeting of probably twelve villages in one of our local pubs and the competition for the cup was launched. I was the first Secretary/Treasurer of the 'Bardfield Cup' with my very able assistant Evelyn who managed the financial side.

It was a big day for the village on Final Day, the game being played on the Great Barfield football pitch. We would get upwards of two thousand spectators. Our home side was a very good team with the Morris brothers and the Patmores Derek and Titch and we won it one year.

There must have been all the village there at the game, upwards of four thousand spectators. The three village pubs were sold out of beer early, it was wonderful and we were in Great Bardfield for thirteen really happy years. In the meantime we had mortgaged ourselves up to the hilt and bought our first property. I now had a German Shepherd dog that I took all over the place showing winning over sixty cards. Heady days

I had moved on from Scribben and Kemp and had got myself a job as a Toolmaker in a trade shop in Chelmsford. I have always been grateful to Ted Sharp and Bill Hobbs for giving me the opportunity of learning a very skilled trade.

After all these years many of the people who have crossed my bows are now no longer with us.

In 1964 Evelyn and I pulled up our roots again and have lived more than half our lives in South Wales. Forty two years to be precise, a life-time for some people.

I have decided to finish this book up to the year 1964, leaving the last forty two years to maybe write about some other day of our life in this beautiful country.

If you will bear with me I do have another humourous story to relate. I came to Wales to work in the pen factory Conway Stewart at Crumlin in the Western Valleys.

The Crumlin Viaduct was still up baffling the engineers. How were they to pull it down. Before they did a film was made called *'Arabesque'* set in the desert with a viaduct dominating the landscape. So they were shooting this desert scene in the heart of the Welsh valleys. The stars were Gregory Peck and one of the most beautiful women in the world Sophia Loren.

The people of the surrounding area were asked to keep away. Gregory Peck was just half way down the hillside on the Swffryd side of the valley watching the filming of an old biplane being flown underneath the viaduct with Sophia Loren halfway along the viaduct. We heard the plane was being piloted by an old retired Major. Then it happened. A young boy slid down to where Mr Peck was sitting. He held his autograph book out to this famous actor who naturally thought he wanted his monica. *'No!'* said the boy *'I want her's pointing to Sophia Loren'*. I bet that did Gregory Peck's ego the world of good.

So those are my memoirs up until 1964. From the London Blitz to India and Burma. Travelling thousands of miles. If the book gets published I hope you enjoy it. I certainly enjoyed relating it.

RONALD WILLIAM DUDLEY

Acknowledgements

An acknowledgement is a thank you for either a service, pleasure, trust or favour given. So I'll start with pleasure and nothing over the past sixty years has given me more pleasure than a lot of people who are now labelled 'LATE' to start with all those brilliant jazz and big band musicians the likes of Sidney Bechet, Louis Armstrong, Harry James, Johnny Hodges. Then there are Clint Eastwood and the 'Duke' John Wayne with their portrayals of Josey Wales (at the present time Mr Eastwood is still with us) and John Wayne as Wooster Cogburn. I love a good western.

So onto the two-legs and four-legs that have given me their trust and loyalty. Three dogs, two cats, over a hundred pigeons, the same amount of cows. Two pedigree bulls of which one was infertile firing blanks for which it was taken to court. Just a small Jersey. The other bull a ton and a half Friesian who had more tadpoles than there are in a farm pond. Not forgetting the fighting cock that you will read about in my book and also two horses, 14 hands George and 18 hands Punch.

So moving on to the acknowledgements for the people who encouraged me to write a book about my experiences of Burma and India during and after WWII. I am a scribe for a weekly racing pigeon journal named The British Homing World and I typed a couple of pages at their request for what the war meant to me. This was followed up by another request of my time in India when the country was waiting for Home Rule. From this I typed a 50 page manuscript read by a few people. I would like to thank these people for their patience in reading the said manuscript. It was a couple of these readers who suggested I approach a publisher which I did. So it's their fault you're lumbered with this book.

I would personally like to thank Pete Flowers who kindly wrote the flattering Foreword for this book.

Lastly to Malcolm Thomas the Books Manager of J.R. Davies (Printers) Limited of Abertillery Gwent, my publisher. Malcolm has given me help and advice, pulling no punches. I thank you all.

A very apt quote: *Tomorrow is the most important thing in life. Comes into us at midnight very clean. It's perfect when it arrives and it puts itself in our hands and hopes we've learnt something from yesterday.*

John Wayne 1907-79

Cockney Rhyming Slang for Beginners

Uncle Ned - Head
Loaf of Bread - Head
Captain's Log - Bog
Todd Sloane - On Your Own
Kate Carney - Army
Rosie Lee - Tea
Tit fer Tat - Hat
Borasic Lint - Skint
Pork Pies (Porkies) - Lies
Plates of Meat - Feet
Abergavenny - A Penny
Brahms and Liszt - Pissed
Daisy Roots - Boots
Alan Whickers - Knickers
Apples an Pears - Stairs
Apple Tart - A Fart
Auntie Nellie - Belly
Bob Hope - Soap
Barnet Fair - Hair
Bath Bun - The Sun
Bell Ringers - Fingers
Betty Grable - Table
Big Dippers - Slippers
Boots and Socks - Pox
Bottle of Beer - Ear
Bow and Quiver - Liver
Butchers Hook - Look
Bubble Gum - Bum
Brussels Sprout - Boy Scout
Bugs Bunny - Money
Button and Bows - Toes
Captain Bligh - Pie
Charles Dance - A Chance
Charing Cross - A Horse
Charlie Pride - A Ride
Christopher Lee - Pee
Clothes Pegs - Legs
Crimea - Beer
Cream Crackered - Knackered
Cough and Stutter - Butter
Cough and Sneeze - Cheese
Conan Doyle - A Boil
Custard and Jelly - The Telly
David Gower - A Shower
Darby Kelly - Belly
Dog and Bone - Phone
Dicky Bird - A Word
Dunlop Tyre - Liar
Duchess of Fyfe - Wife
Fiddle and Flute - Suit
Farmer Giles - Piles
Fridge Freezer - Geezer
Frog and Toad - Road
Gary Glitter - Pint of Bitter
Hampstead Heath - Teeth
Herring and Kipper - Stripper
Hush Puppy - A Yuppie
Irish Stew - True
Gypsy Rose Lee - Tea
Jam Jar - Car
Jagger's Lips - Chips
Jack Jones - On Ones Own
Jimmy Skinner - Dinner
Jimmy Riddle - Piddle
Jimmy Nail - Stale
Jellied Eels - Wheels
John Wayne - Train
John Major - A Wager
Joe Blake - Steak
Joanna - Piano
Jockey's Whip - A Kip (sleep)
King Canutes - Boots
Judi Dench - Stench
Jolly Rodger - Lodger
Lady Godiva - A Fiver
La-Do-Dah - A Car
Kipper and Plaice - Face
Kings and Queens - Baked Beans
King Death - Bad Breath
Lemon Curd - Turd
Lee Marvin - Starving
Little and Large - Marge
Loop the Loop - Soup
Merchant Banker - Wanker
Max Walls - Balls
Mahatma Gandhi - Brandy

Pony - Twenty Five Pounds
Mutt and Jeff - Deaf
Mother Kelly - Belly
Monkey's Cousin - A Dozen
Moby Dick - Feel Sick
Mince Pies - Eyes
Nervous Wreck - Cheque
Nat King Cole - The Dole
Mutter and Stutter - Butter
North and South - Mouth
Orinoco - Cocoa
Oxo Cube - The London Tube
Philharmonic - Gin and Tonic
Pen and Ink - Stink
Pat Cash - A Slash
Pat and Mick - Sick
Port and Brandy - Randy
Pigs Ear - Beer
Pie and Liquor - The Vicar
Raquel Welch - A Belch
Raspberry Ripple - A Nipple
Puff and Drag - A Fag
Rock of Ages - Wages
Rock'n'Roll - The Dole
Rising Damp - The Cramp
Rhythm and Blues - Shoes
Rub-a-Dub - The Pub
Royal Navy - Gravy
Round the Houses - Trousers
Rosie O'Grady's - The Ladies
Rosie Lee - Tea
Rory O'Moore - Floor
Ronnie Biggs - Digs
Sebastian Coe - Toe
Sky Rocket - Toe
Skin and Blister - Sister
Starsky and Hutch - Crutch
Stanner and Stutter - Butter
Sodom and Gomorrah - To Borrow
Steve McQueens - Jeans
Almond Rocks - Socks
Swallow and Sigh - Tie
Dickie Dirt - Shirt
Tea Leaf - A Thief
Tom and Dick - Sick
Tod Sloane - On One's Own
Tin Tack - The Sack
Trouble and Strife - Wife
Tom Sawyer - A Lawyer
Uncle Bert - Shirt
Two Eyes of Blue - Too True
Two by Four - Whore
Wallace and Gromit - Vomit
Vera Lynn - Gin
Wicked Rumours - Bloomers
Whistel and Fluter - Suit
Wyatt Earp - A Burp
Bristol or Manchester Cities - Titties
Pony and Trap - Crap
Alan Minter - Printer
Pie and Mash - Slash